QUALITY JOBS AND THE FUTURE OF WORK IN ASIA AND THE PACIFIC

IMPACTS OF A TRIPLE TRANSITION—
DEMOGRAPHIC, DIGITAL, AND GREEN

SEPTEMBER 2024

ASIAN DEVELOPMENT BANK

 Creative Commons Attribution 3.0 IGO license (CC BY 3.0 IGO)

© 2024 Asian Development Bank
6 ADB Avenue, Mandaluyong City, 1550 Metro Manila, Philippines
Tel +63 2 8632 4444; Fax +63 2 8636 2444
www.adb.org

Some rights reserved. Published in 2024.

ISBN 978-92-9270-892-4 (print); 978-92-9270-893-1 (PDF); 978-92-9270-894-8 (ebook)
Publication Stock No. TCS240444-2
DOI: http://dx.doi.org/10.22617/TCS240444-2

The views expressed in this publication are those of the authors and do not necessarily reflect the views and policies of the Asian Development Bank (ADB) or its Board of Governors or the governments they represent.

ADB does not guarantee the accuracy of the data included in this publication and accepts no responsibility for any consequence of their use. The mention of specific companies or products of manufacturers does not imply that they are endorsed or recommended by ADB in preference to others of a similar nature that are not mentioned.

By making any designation of or reference to a particular territory or geographic area in this document, ADB does not intend to make any judgments as to the legal or other status of any territory or area.

This publication is available under the Creative Commons Attribution 3.0 IGO license (CC BY 3.0 IGO) https://creativecommons.org/licenses/by/3.0/igo/. By using the content of this publication, you agree to be bound by the terms of this license. For attribution, translations, adaptations, and permissions, please read the provisions and terms of use at https://www.adb.org/terms-use#openaccess.

This CC license does not apply to non-ADB copyright materials in this publication. If the material is attributed to another source, please contact the copyright owner or publisher of that source for permission to reproduce it. ADB cannot be held liable for any claims that arise as a result of your use of the material.

Please contact pubsmarketing@adb.org if you have questions or comments with respect to content, or if you wish to obtain copyright permission for your intended use that does not fall within these terms, or for permission to use the ADB logo.

Corrigenda to ADB publications may be found at http://www.adb.org/publications/corrigenda.

Notes:
In this publication, "$" refers to United States dollars.
ADB recognizes "Korean" as referring to the Republic of Korea and "Vietnam" as Viet Nam.

Cover design by Cleone Flores Baradas.

Contents

Tables, Figures, and Boxes	iv
Acknowledgments	v
Abbreviations	vi
Executive Summary	vii
1 Introduction	**1**
2 Effects of Megatrends on Job Creation and Job Quality	**3**
A Triple Transition	3
Job Quantity and Labor Demand	6
Job Quality and Skills	21
Job Structures and Social Protection	26
Confluence: The Effects of Intersections	31
3 Policy Considerations	**33**
The Role of Policy and Markets	33
An Intersectional Policy Approach	35
The Context Effect	39
4 Conclusion	**41**
References	**42**

Tables, Figures, and Boxes

Tables

1	Demographic Trends in Association of Southeast Asian Nations+6 Countries	9
2	Overview of Changes to Demand for Skills Resulting from the Triple Transition	22
3	Key Linkages Between Megatrends Affecting Labor Demand	32
4	Individuals' Readiness for the Digital Economy—Network Readiness Index People Ranking of Highest- and Lowest-Performing Economies in the Region	38

Figures

1	Median Age of the Labor Force in Selected Asia and Pacific Countries, 1990, 2000, 2010, 2020, and 2030	6
2	Share of Population Aged 0–14, 15–64, and 65 and Above in Asia and the Pacific, 1950–2097 (Projected)	8
3	Mobile Internet Connectivity in East Asia and the Pacific, 2017–2022	10
4	Economic Losses from Climate Change in Developing Asia Under a High-Emissions Scenario by 2100	17
5	Working Hours Lost to Heat Stress, By Sector and By Sub-Region, Asia and the Pacific, 1995 and 2030 (Projections)	21
6	Availability of Digital Human Capital, by Country-Income Grouping, 2021	24
7	Institutional Barriers to Fourth Industrial Revolution Training Delivery and Curricula Updating—Results of an ADB-Commissioned Survey in Bangladesh, Georgia, and Indonesia	25
8	Labor Productivity and Social Protection Expenditure, Selected Countries, 2019	27
9	Share of Population 65 and Above Still in the Labor Force By Gender, Selected Economies, 2021	28
10	A Framework for Adaptive Social Protection to Strengthen Livelihoods Resilience	30
11	Technology Adoption by Log Gross Domestic Product for Selected Countries, 2021	40

Boxes

1	Growth, Jobs, and Productivity	2
2	The Economies of the Triple Transition in Asia and the Pacific	4
3	Definitions of Digital Jobs	11
4	Gig Work Preferences Among Youth and Employers in Three Asian Economies— Results of an ADB-Commissioned Survey	15
5	Definitions of Green Jobs	18
6	Extending Social Protection Coverage to Self-Employed Gig Workers	29
7	Skilling and Social Protection for the Triple Transition	34

Acknowledgments

This report was prepared as part of the work program of the Social Development Team, Human and Social Development Sector Office, Sectors Group (SG-HSD) of the Asian Development Bank (ADB). It was funded under ADB regional technical assistance, Quality Jobs and the Future of Work, which aims to strengthen the capacity of developing member countries to facilitate access to quality jobs through new directions for social protection in labor markets, and effective approaches for skills development and job facilitation.

Helen Osborne, SG-HSD consultant, was lead author of the final report. PricewaterhouseCoopers LLP (PwC), India led the research and produced outputs that formed the basis of this report. Duncan Campbell, SG-HSD consultant, contributed to the analysis presented in this report. Peer review was by Paul Vandenberg, principal economist, Economic Research and Development Impact Department, ADB. Oleksiy (Alex) Ivaschenko, senior social protection and jobs specialist, SG-HSD, oversaw the project and provided review and guidance for the report, with the support and overall supervision of Wendy Walker, director, SG-HSD.

Abbreviations

ADB	Asian Development Bank
AI	artificial intelligence
ASEAN	Association of Southeast Asian Nations
GDP	gross domestic product
GHG	greenhouse gas
ICT	information and communication technology
ILO	International Labour Organization
IMF	International Monetary Fund
LTC	long-term care
OECD	Organisation for Economic Co-operation and Development
PRC	People's Republic of China
PwC	PricewaterhouseCoopers
UNESCAP	United Nations Economic and Social Commission for Asia and the Pacific
WEF	World Economic Forum

Executive Summary

The structures of production and consumption are being reshaped through the transformative effects of various "megatrends," with major implications for jobs. Three megatrends are the subject of this study: (i) aging and demographic transition, (ii) Fourth Industrial Revolution and digital transition, and (iii) climate change and green transition. In Asia and the Pacific, the nature of this "triple transition" is distinct. While the megatrends are simultaneous, they are occurring in the region at different speeds and from different starting points across geographies. **This report assesses the effects of the three megatrends on job creation and job quality in Asia and the Pacific.** The main focus is on labor demand. Job quality is confined to two dimensions: skill endowment and social protection coverage. The report aims to strengthen the policy focus on the critical intersection of megatrends to guide a more integrated approach to policymaking for the triple transition.

Labor Demand and Demographic Transition

Changing population structures affect demand in the care sector. Care dependency ratios in the region are set to almost double, particularly for older persons (aged 65 years and above) in aging economies. More care jobs will be needed. Many are low-wage, informal, and precarious. A particular growth area is in long-term care services (LTC), such as home-based eldercare. In Singapore, a 130% increase in demand for long-term care direct-care workers is projected to 2030 from 2017.

As societies age, demand is likely to shift from durable goods (such as cars) to services (such as health care) due to consumption preferences of older people. Smaller households use more energy per capita. Households with more children or older people have different resource allocation priorities, for example, the former will tend to prioritize education expenditure.

As the median age of the labor force shifts upward, at some point average productivity begins to decline. Output will decline if there are fewer workers not offset by an increase in productivity, and output per capita will decline as the age composition of the labor force becomes older and less productive. "Demographic drag" (where labor productivity growth slows down with aging) is greater in emerging than in advanced economies.

Labor Demand and Digital Transition

Technological disruptions lead to a reallocation of workers and jobs, i.e., greater structural labor market churn. Churn rates in the region range from 19% in Hong Kong, China to 30% in Pakistan. The latest digital advancements are affecting jobs differently compared to earlier stages of automation. The future demand for labor cannot be fully known, as technologies continue to evolve and their full range of uses is a process of discovery.

Technologies that result in job loss but also higher productivity and lower costs may lead to higher job-creating growth in a general equilibrium sense. Furthermore, a digitally networked economy implies a major reduction in transaction costs, eliminating barriers of time and distance, leading to a more efficient intermediation between labor supply and demand. A 1-percentage-point increase in the digitalization of the People's Republic of China (PRC) economy is associated with a 0.3-percentage-point growth in gross domestic product (GDP).

Digitalization is also transforming the way people engage with employment, through more gig work. The past decade has seen a fivefold increase in the number of digital labor platforms globally, particularly in redundant web-based and location-based platforms (where tasks are conducted in person in a specific geographic location, such as taxi driving and domestic work). Gig work is generally performed by young people (aged 35 years or below), six in 10 online gig workers live in smaller cities, and much gig work is informal and unprotected.

Labor Demand and Green Transition

Job estimates are net positive for climate change mitigation scenarios. They vary depending on modeling parameters. The Asian Development Bank (ADB) estimated the impacts of a $172 billion, five-part green growth strategy that can generate 30 million jobs in Southeast Asia by 2030. Overall, renewable energy technologies are currently more labor-intensive than fossil fuel technologies.

The redistributive job effects of the green transition are significant. The reshaping of labor markets will displace some workers and create new opportunities for others. There can be a temporal lag, with job losses preceding job gains, as well as increased spatial and income inequalities. People with lower levels of educational attainment and skills mainly work in polluting jobs. Transitioning from a nongreen to a green job is particularly challenging for all workers.

Climate change is itself increasingly a determinant of economic opportunity. If people are already vulnerable, the climate effects compound with other non-climatic stressors of vulnerability, such as poverty, poor health, or weak infrastructure, to disrupt livelihoods. It is estimated that rising temperatures can lead to a global loss of productivity equivalent to 80 million full-time jobs.

Job Quality and Skills

The megatrends imply an upward skill bias in the demand for labor. The likelihood of skill obsolescence increases relative to age. Skills in greatest demand in the medium-term future are a mix of technical skills—related to demand in the care, digital, and green economies—and soft skills. In particular, the nonroutine and cognitive nature of new jobs emphasizes the importance of higher-order cognitive (soft) skills.

In digital labor markets, it is increasingly the possession of skills, not qualifications, that matters. Digital skills are of increasing relevance to the economic value (at least) of education, with acquisition expanding through alternative, nonformal education channels, such as boot camps. In emerging fields like cybersecurity and robotics, advanced skills are required, but not necessarily advanced degrees, in so-called "new collar" jobs.

Skills play an important role in technology adoption, which can affect the pace of transformation through the triple transition. A skills shortage to adapt to changing labor demand creates a brake on the pace of the structural transformation that the changes imply. A key issue in addressing the digital skills shortage is an "institutional bottleneck": a skills shortage in teachers and trainers equipped to impart relevant digital skills in demand by employers.

Adaptation ("greening") of existing skill sets appears to be a quantitatively greater skills agenda than the acquisition of entirely new skills focusing on core green technologies, such as renewable energy. New skills associated with core green technologies will be at the medium or advanced skill level, both for existing and for incoming workers.

Skills required for work are constantly changing in line with shifting labor demand. Of existing "core skills" demanded by employers at the high end of the occupational spectrum of employees, 44% will change over the next 5 years. Such change means "learnability" becomes a core capability for work, understood as "the ability and willingness to learn to unlearn and relearn."

Job Structures and Social Protection

Social protection enables economic change to occur. Social protection spending is correlated with increased labor productivity (Figure 8, p.27). Providing resilience speeds a return to growth from socioeconomic shock or structural disruption and at lower social cost.

The demographic transition is challenging the solvency of social protection systems. A decline in new entrants to the labor force in the context of increasing longevity, i.e., in the relative size of the working-age population, depletes the resources of contributory-based pension systems.

Meanwhile, the digital transition generates new categories of workers that need access to social protection. Traditionally, work has provided security if people are formally employed. If gig workers are self-employed (e.g., not classified as employees of the platform that mediates their participation in the labor market), access to social protection can only be delivered through other ways than an employment relationship.

Climate change creates new dynamics of livelihood vulnerabilities that need to be met by appropriate social protection. Growing numbers of people in the region will not be able to meet their basic needs without external support. Support to learn and adopt behaviors and practices that facilitate adaptation toward climate-resilient livelihoods is central to a just transition to a greener economy where no one is left behind.

Confluence: The Effects of Intersections

The ways the megatrends coexist and overlap ultimately determine the type and size of their effects. Typically, megatrends are studied in isolation, yet it is their combined effects that will shape the future quantity and quality of jobs. Evidence is limited about the intersections of megatrends, which leaves uncertainty for governments in cost–benefit planning. The report maps some key linkages between megatrends, as discussed in the literature. These linkages are focused on labor demand, per the main variable of interest in this study. Examples are set out in the following table:

Table: Examples of Linkages Between Megatrends Affecting Labor Demand

Demographic transition ↔ Digital transition		
Automation can offset the negative effects of population aging on productivity.	Growth in the gig economy increases demand for workers who prioritize flexibility, including younger and older workers.	Innovation in health tech for longevity will create and disrupt jobs.
Digital transition ↔ Green transition		
Digitalization is a route for less carbon-intensive production, consumption, and work.	The transition to renewable energy requires both digital and power electronics technologies—shifting labor demand.	Digital innovations can help support climate-vulnerable workers, for example, artificial intelligence applications for farmers.
Green transition ↔ Demographic transition		
Aging—and smaller household sizes—contribute to moderately increased energy consumption per capita—inducing shifts in labor markets.	As populations grow, demand for food increases and consumption preferences can change, with implications for jobs in agriculture (as well as use of natural resources).	Climate change makes work conditions more challenging, especially for older (and other vulnerable) workers exposed to increasing heat waves and other stressors.

Source: Authors' own elaboration.

A New Policy Approach

The effects of megatrends are not predetermined; the policy agenda is an important determinant of outcomes. Yet, the prevailing agenda is too narrow and siloed. Policy dialogue tends to be mainly built from assessing megatrends separately. It is also centered on skilling and social protection, without enough focus on labor demand. A new jobs-focused, intersectional policy approach by governments will enable policymaking that maximizes the benefits (and minimizes the risks) from how the megatrends overlap and combine. The job gains from an integrated policy response to megatrends can be significant.

Policy design and implementation should be flexible to the differentiated diffusion of megatrends and adaptation capacity (or "readiness") among countries. Such differentiated policymaking requires a new set of composite instruments capable of combining insights from the intersections of megatrends to identify opportunities for efficiency gains, impact multipliers, and crosscutting interventions.

Policy Shifts

The following four policy shifts will help governments adopt a more intersectional policy approach to address the labor market impacts of megatrends:

Policy shift 1: Create a jobs-centered approach to megatrends.

Governments need an intentional and coordinated jobs-centered policy agenda for the triple transition. The policy objective should shift from economic growth per se to inclusive and sustainable growth centered on quality jobs for productivity.

Policy example: Korean New Deal, 2020 (New Deal 2.0 updated 2021)

Policy shift 2: Strengthen capacity to anticipate changing labor demand.

Policy systems and institutions for the triple transition need to be agile and flexible in step with evolving labor market demand. The new normal in policymaking is uncertainty, which calls for anticipatory planning, not least because changes in labor demand lag changes in growth.

Policy example: Centre for Strategic Futures, Prime Minister's Office, Singapore

Policy shift 3: Understand distributional impacts of megatrends on people and jobs.

The triple transition calls for strengthened policy capabilities in shaping human-centered responses. Governments need policy approaches that assess and cater to the highly differentiated experiences of individual workers faced with job disruptions due to megatrends.

Policy example: Network Readiness Index, Portulans Institute and University of Oxford Saïd Business School, global

Policy shift 4: Focus on productivity enhancement of informal workers.

The success of the policy response to the triple transition should be measured by improvements to the productivity of the majority informal workforce of the region. Without intentional policy action, the effects of the megatrends may worsen labor underutilization and low productivity. It is important to avoid a reform package that will only benefit more educated workers in the formal labor market.

Policy example: Association of Southeast Asian Nations (ASEAN) Labor Productivity Index

1 Introduction

The structures of production and consumption are being reshaped through the transformative effects of various "megatrends," with major implications for jobs. Three megatrends are the subject of this study:[1] (i) aging and demographic transition, (ii) Fourth Industrial Revolution and digital transition, and (iii) climate change and green transition. In Asia and the Pacific, the nature of these megatrends is distinct compared with other regions, with specific implications for the creation and quality of jobs.[2]

Already in the region, structural weaknesses in labor markets are limiting the economic and social gains from growth. Even before the setbacks to poverty and inequality precipitated by the coronavirus disease (COVID-19) pandemic, high growth rates were not translating into improved labor market participation and productivity (Box 1). Two-thirds of the region's labor force work informally. Typically, informal work is precarious, with low and irregular pay, and lacking social protection. This share of informal work is over three times higher on average in the developing and emerging economies of Asia (71%) than in the advanced economies (22%).[3] The majority of informal workers are self-employed, yet it is wage employment that is correlated with quality work.[4]

Addressing quality jobs deficits is a major policy concern to unlock the region's potential, and the increasing and uncertain impacts that megatrends are having on socioeconomic structures makes the policy response both more pressing and more complex. While there is an opportunity for governments and other actors to harness these dynamics to generate more and better jobs, there is growing evidence of the risk that prevailing labor market weaknesses will become further entrenched. In particular, that many future jobs will be informal and precarious.

> There is growing evidence of the risk that prevailing labor market weaknesses will become further entrenched. In particular, that many future jobs will be informal and precarious.

---

[1] Megatrends are those trends which are disruptive of economic and social norms and structures that portend a secular shift in the status quo; the opposite of a passing trend. The Oxford English Dictionary defines a megatrend as "an important shift in the progress of a society or of any other particular field or activity" (oed.com).

[2] For example, Asia and the Pacific is aging faster than any other region; Asia is the world's largest market for industrial robots; and 75% of Asia and the Pacific's GDP is exposed to climate disruption.

[3] International Labour Organization (ILO). 2022. *Asia–Pacific Employment and Social Outlook 2022: Rethinking Sectoral Strategies for a Human-Centred Future of Work*. https://www.ilo.org/wcmsp5/groups/public/---dgreports/---dcomm/---publ/documents/publication/wcms_862410.pdf.

[4] S. Hovhavnisyan et al. 2022. Global Job Quality. *World Bank Working Paper* 10134. This global study used multiple indicators to measure job quality and found: "a strong positive correlation between the JQM [Job Quality Measure] and the share of the wage employed in total employment across developing countries, indicating that countries with more opportunities for workers to find paid employment perform better in terms of the availability of good jobs than countries with large self-employed or informal worker populations."

> **Box 1: Growth, Jobs, and Productivity**
>
> Since 2015, the economies of Asia and the Pacific have made very limited progress to meet Sustainable Development Goal (SDG) 8, which aims to *"promote sustained, inclusive and sustainable economic growth, full and productive employment and decent work for all."*[a] During that time, the region was a major contributor to global growth (57% from 2015 to 2021).[b] Despite expanding output, corresponding levels of quality jobs have not been created.[c] The effects of economic growth on the creation of productive employment is not only contingent on the rate of growth, but also on how efficiently growth translates into quality jobs.[d] In turn, this can depend on which sectors employ the most people, and capital- or labor-intensive different sectors are as factors of production. Growth has been employment-poor, for example, in much of Central Asia, or other economies that rely on primary commodity exports for growth. These industries are highly capital-intensive and little embedded in the rest of the economy.
>
> It is predicted that *"the era of global GDP growth fueled by population numbers is coming to an end."* Over the next 40 years, only 9% of growth will come from a population-fueled increase in labor supply, compared to a 56% contribution in the period 1975–2000.[e] Future growth will rely on productivity increase. This in turn depends on labor quality, not mere factor accumulation. Ultimately, employment and growth benefits are maximized when productivity and incomes of workers are raised. Labor income is the principal component of aggregate demand. Conversely, weak labor markets have compounding negative effects on growth. For example, in the Pacific nations, in general, there are relatively large youth populations, yet constrained domestic labor markets. A lack of viable jobs locally leads to high rates of out-migration, which puts a downward spiral on earnings, consumption, and growth.
>
> [a] Similarly, low progress has been made in the region on SDGs 6, 12, 14, and 17. UNESCAP. 2023. *Asia and the Pacific SDG Progress Report 2023: Championing Sustainability Despite Adversities.* https://www.unescap.org/kp/2023/asia-and-pacific-sdg-progress-report-2023.
> [b] Seong, J. et al. 2023. Asia on the cusp of a new era. Mckinsey Global Institute. 22 September. https://www.mckinsey.com/mgi/our-research/asia-on-the-cusp-of-a-new-era.
> [c] The relationship between growth and job creation is measured by employment intensity. Employment intensity is the extent job creation increases if an economy expands its output. So, if growth goes up by 1%, the amount of employment growth that results can be measured. Alongside other labor market indicators, such as unemployment rates or employment-to-population ratios, it is another useful measure of the macroeconomic performance of a country.
> [d] ILO. *Employment-rich Economic Growth.* https://www.ilo.org/global/topics/dw4sd/themes/employment-rich/lang--en/index.htm.
> [e] A. Mason and R. Lee. 2022. Six Ways Population Change Will Affect the Global Economy. *Population and Development Review.* Vol. 48, Issue 1. pp. 51-73. https://onlinelibrary.wiley.com/doi/10.1111/padr.12469.

This report assesses the effects of the three megatrends on job creation and job quality in Asia and the Pacific. The main focus is on labor demand. Job quality is confined to two dimensions: skill endowment and social protection coverage. The report aims to strengthen the policy focus on the critical intersection of megatrends to guide a more integrated approach to policymaking for the triple transition. Typically, megatrends are studied in isolation and recommendations derived accordingly. Highlighting the determining role that policy can play in shaping inclusive and sustainable markets for quality jobs, the report sets out four policy shifts for governments to consider in their response to megatrends. It emphasizes the need for flexible and differentiated approaches depending on the stage of diffusion of megatrends and adaptation capacity (or "readiness") among countries.

2 Effects of Megatrends on Job Creation and Job Quality

A Triple Transition

This study focuses on three megatrends that will have major and distinct effects on the labor markets of Asia and the Pacific. The region is undergoing a "triple transition" in the form of (i) demographic transition, (ii) digital transition, and (iii) green transition. The demographic transition is characterized by diversity in the pace of aging, resulting from improvements in education, technology, and human development; the digital transition by the application of advanced digital technologies, such as machine learning and generative artificial intelligence (AI); and the green transition by a more acute level of climate change, with rising planetary temperatures and more frequent weather-related shocks.

While the megatrends are simultaneous, they are occurring in the region at different speeds and from different starting points across geographies. For example, many Pacific nations have young populations, while most Asian economies are rapidly aging or are already aged. As digitalization accelerates, countries engaged in the advanced gig economy continue to have limited electrification and connectivity in some areas. The very varied natural endowments and topography of countries determine their respective climate vulnerability.[5]

The megatrends are transforming socioeconomic structures—the underlying processes of production and consumption and people's behaviors within those. Pathways to growth are shifting toward demographic inclusivity,[6] digital interconnectivity, and environmental sustainability. Production and consumption are restructuring to enable healthy longevity, with more focus on social and economic inclusion (demographic transition). General purpose digital technologies are being applied to all areas of economic (e.g., trade) and social (e.g., communication) activity, helping to make production and consumption more connected and efficient (digital transition). Economic and social activity is becoming more sustainable, through low-carbon processes and protection of natural resources (green transition).

> "Pathways to growth are shifting toward demographic inclusivity, digital interconnectivity, and environmental sustainability."

---

[5] The three megatrends further interconnect with other prevailing structural socioeconomic dynamics that are both push-and-pull factors of change, such as urbanization, globalization, and migration; as well as short-term disruptions, such as economic shocks and conflicts.

[6] Demographic inclusivity refers to growth that maximizes opportunities for economic inclusion of all people, regardless of vulnerabilities, including age-related.

The shifts in production and consumption influence patterns of job loss and job creation. New sectors, occupations, roles, and tasks emerge, others become redundant and are destroyed, while many evolve and reorient. In particular, new economic clusters emerge from the megatrends, which change the demand for labor: the care economy, the digital economy, and the green economy (Box 2). In part, new growth and employment opportunities are generated through market forces (private); in part, they are initiated and accelerated through policy agendas (public). The diffusion of infrastructure and of innovation is based in the economics of what is feasible, not only what is technologically possible, shaped by the regulatory and policy environment.

Box 2: The Economies of the Triple Transition in Asia and the Pacific

The care economy.[a] Along with health care, the care economy recognizes caregiving as a vital function in economies to enable a healthy and productive workforce, and active aging. Paid work in the care economy can be formal or informal. It is predominantly low-skilled, distinct from a niche of specialist jobs. Much care work is unpaid and unrecognized in labor market terms, such as labor rights and employment statistics, and unaccounted for in the country's gross domestic product (GDP). Of unpaid women care workers who live with care recipients in Bangladesh, 94% work informally.[b] On average, close to 50% of unpaid caregivers are classified as out of the labor force, the highest share being in poorer countries such as Timor-Leste (69%) and Pakistan (88%). In more developed countries, paid care is a fast-growing sector. Taking a developed country as an indicator of growth potential, in the United States, estimates have valued the paid-care economy higher ($648 billion) than the domestic pharmaceutical industry ($510 billion), and than the hotel, car manufacturing, and social networking industries combined.

The digital economy. The digital economy is built on "networks of economic activities, commercial transactions, and professional interactions … enabled by information and communications technologies (ICT)." Importantly for labor demand, the digital economy combines established digital industries and non-digital industries, enabling their production, i.e., industries from which digital industries require inputs and to which they provide output.[c] Based on input–output modeling in 16 economies of Asia and the Pacific, their respective domestic digital economy is estimated to account for 2%–9% of GDP. Ranges increase from 17% to 35% of GDP when a broader definition of a "digitally-dependent economy" is applied, which accounts for forward- and backward-linkages to sectors that are critically dependent on core digital sectors.

The green economy. The green economy is defined as "low carbon, resource efficient, and socially inclusive." In a green economy, "economic activities, infrastructure, and assets… allow reduced carbon emissions and pollution, enhanced energy and resource efficiency, and prevention of the loss of biodiversity and ecosystem services."[d] The size of the green economy is often measured in terms of projected need to meet climate goals, rather than current contribution to output. ADB estimated in 2021 that around $1.5 trillion annually is required in the region from 2016 to 2030 to green economies and meet the Sustainable Development Goals.[e] An earlier study found that Asia outperforms other regions in sales, exports, and patenting of Low-Carbon Environmental Goods and Services (LCEGS),[f] although relatively developed countries contribute most.[g]

continued on next page

Box 2 continued

^a Some definitions of the care economy are broad and encompass all health and social work and education sectors. (ILO. 2018. *Care Work and Care Jobs for the Future of Decent Work*. https://www.ilo.org/wcmsp5/groups/public/---dgreports/---dcomm/---publ/documents/publication/wcms_633135.pdf; UN Economist Network. New Economics for Sustainable Development. Purple Economy (Care Economy+). https://www.un.org/sites/un2.un.org/files/purple_economy_14_march.pdf.). Childcare and eldercare are two key components for workers, as well as care for people who are sick or who have disabilities, and include indirect care such as domestic duties of cleaning and cooking. In effect, care is a public good for economic activity.

^b In upper-middle-income countries such as the People's Republic of China (PRC), this share is 56%. Based on analysis of the employment status of female, unpaid caregivers in urban areas, relatively richer countries such as Brunei Darussalam, the PRC, Thailand, and Viet Nam have close to 70% of care workers who are employed, but at low wages. In the Association of Southeast Asian Nations or ASEAN, much home-based care of the young, older persons, and people with disabilities is provided by domestic workers, many of whom are migrant workers and are informal.

^c ADB. 2021. *Capturing the Digital Economy: A Proposed Measurement Framework and Its Applications. A Special Supplement to Key Indicators for Asia and the Pacific 2021*. https://www.adb.org/sites/default/files/publication/722366/capturing-digital-economy-measurement-framework.pdf.

^d UN Environment Programme. Green Economy. https://www.unep.org/regions/asia-and-pacific/regional-initiatives/supporting-resource-efficiency/green-economy.

^e ADB. Asia and the Pacific's Green Economic Reset: 12 Things to Know. https://www.adb.org/news/videos/asia-and-pacific-s-green-economic-reset-12-things-know.

^f Low-Carbon Environmental Goods and Services is a United Kingdom classification for environmental sectors. https://www.data.gov.uk/dataset/ab9e8025-9d00-4172-b0e9-9262967e70b6/low-carbon-and-environmental-goods-and-services-industry-analysis.

^g S. Fankhauser, A. Kazaglis, and S. Srivastav. 2017. Green Growth Opportunities for Asia. *ADB Economics Working Paper Series*. No. 508. ADB. https://www.adb.org/sites/default/files/publication/224391/ewp-508.pdf.

The geography and inclusivity of jobs also shift. For example, if out-migration of young workers drives net increase in population aging in a rural or coastal community, demand for eldercare services will rise (demographic transition). Mainly men work in polluting jobs, and women are underrepresented in green-task jobs. People with lower levels of educational attainment and skills also mainly work in polluting jobs, and are less likely to take part in training (green transition).[7] Furthermore, the three transitions also change the ways in which people engage with the labor market. New concepts emerge about what it means to have a "quality" job, such as one that is environmentally responsible, or adequately protected outside of a traditional employment relationship.

The following section presents the labor market impacts of the triple transition. It focuses on what the megatrends mean for jobs in quantitative terms, then turns to skills and social protection, as two indicators of job quality. Labor demand is the primary variable. First, what are the effects on job creation, destruction, and reallocation? Second, will future jobs be higher skilled? And third, what do changes mean for social protection? Each of the three megatrends are discussed in turn along these three analytical dimensions.

---

[7] OECD. 2023. *Job Creation and Local Economic Development 2023: Bridging the Great Green Divide*. OECD Publishing. https://doi.org/10.1787/21db61c1-en. This research defined green-task jobs based on the O-NET taxonomy of greenness of tasks for over 900 occupations, and analyzed current and projected green-task jobs at subregional level in 30 OECD countries.

Job Quantity and Labor Demand

Labor Demand and Demographic Transition

The median age of populations is projected to rise in all countries of Asia and the Pacific. Population aging—a rise in the median age of the population—is being caused by (i) older people enjoying longer lives and (ii) a decline in the fertility rate. These are signs of global progress through economic development, increases in income, and advances in education and health care. Populations are aging both absolutely and relatively. This means the workforce is getting older, increasing steadily in all countries—as illustrated by a selection of countries in Figure 1.

Demographic transition has direct, indirect, and aggregate effects on labor demand. The direct effects are on demand for the care economy (Box 2, p. 4). The indirect effects occur through changing consumption patterns of older or younger consumers. Older people are "dis-savers" on aggregate. They sell assets, rather than invest, and their consumption is not in equity purchases, such as the housing market. Further, demographic transition shapes the size and productivity of the workforce available to meet labor demand. This can also have sector effects on labor supply due to age-related work capabilities. For example, there is a lower share of older workers in the construction sector.

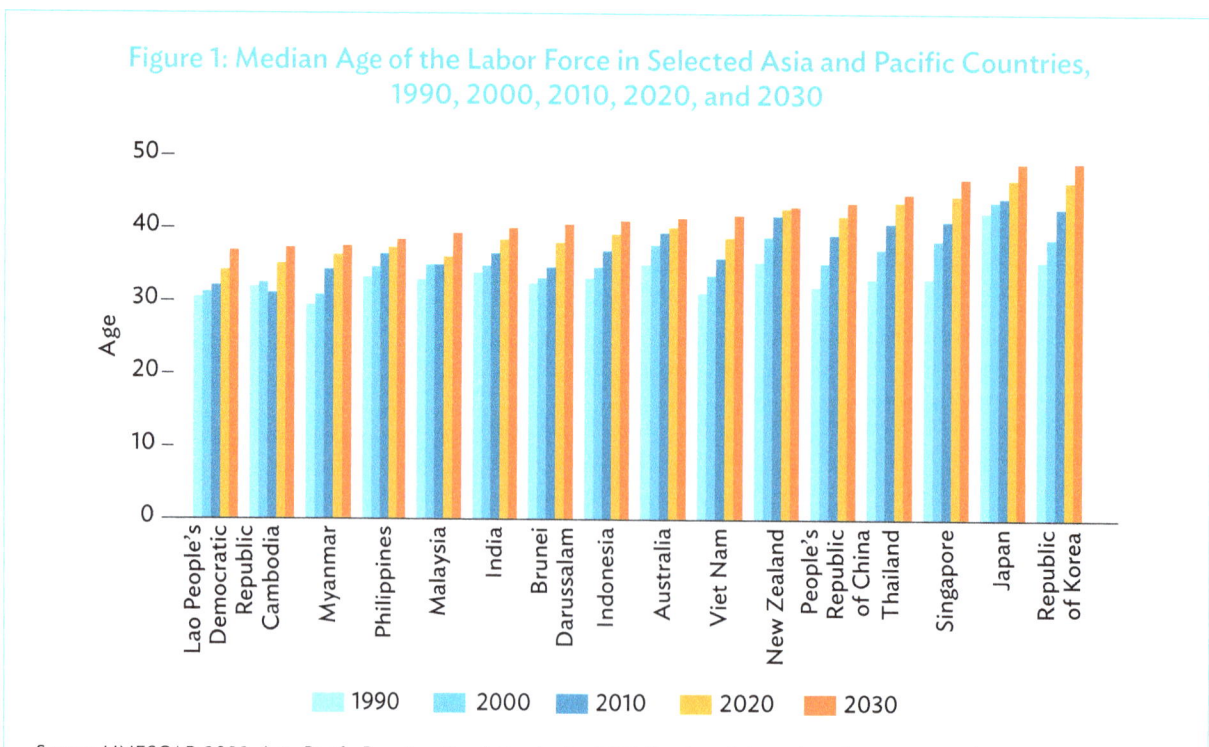

Figure 1: Median Age of the Labor Force in Selected Asia and Pacific Countries, 1990, 2000, 2010, 2020, and 2030

Source: UNESCAP. 2022. *Asia-Pacific Report on Population Ageing 2022: Trends, policies and good practices regarding older persons and population ageing*. https://www.unescap.org/sites/default/d8files/knowledge-products/AP-Ageing-2022-report.pdf. Data taken from ILO. 2018. *Preparing for the Future of Work. National Policy Responses in ASEAN+6*; and ILO. 2021. *Getting Older: Confronting Asia and the Pacific's Ageing Labour Force*. https://www.ilo.org/asia/media-centre/news/WCMS_818956/lang--en/index.htm.

Changing population structures affect demand in the care sector. Care dependency ratios in the region, particularly for older persons (aged 65 years and above) in aging economies, are set to almost double.[8] More care jobs will be needed.[9] Expanding childcare, parental leave, and long-term care (LTC) services can create up to 299 million jobs worldwide by 2035, assuming investment of $5.4 trillion annually (equivalent to 4.2% of total annual gross domestic product).[10] It is estimated that Thailand will need 2–3.4 million primary-care workers and caregivers in household services, childcare, and eldercare by 2030, and 2.4–4.7 million by 2050.[11] A particular growth area is in LTC services, such as home-based eldercare. In Singapore, a 130% increase in demand for LTC direct-care workers is projected to 2030 since 2017.[12] Typically, the care sector is low-wage, informal, and female-dominant. Most likely, informal female care work will rise. If more and better care jobs are created, more women will be able to join the workforce.[13] Promoting healthy aging will also spur growth in demand for specialist, formal jobs in medical science related to gerontology and the health-care industry, in general. A significant increase in health workers is projected globally by 2030, although there are geographic disparities in meeting demand, with small island developing states facing particular shortages.[14]

As societies age, demand is likely to shift from durable goods (such as cars) to services (such as health care). This results from consumption preferences of older people. Changing composition of households due to demographic transition can also have sector impacts, with knock-on effects on jobs. Smaller households use more energy per capita. Households with more children or older people have different resource allocation priorities, for example, the former will tend to prioritize education expenditure. Pakistan is among countries with the highest share of intergenerational living.[15] Age-related work capabilities can also drive labor shortages. For example, there is a lower share of older workers in construction or other physically taxing occupations.

Demographic transition also affects aggregate labor demand. Population size and composition serve as fundamental drivers of an economy's potential for aggregate growth and productivity, which in turn drives aggregate demand—including for labor. The ratio of people of working age (aged 15–64 years, i.e., the working-age population) to non-contributing children and older people sets the limits for economic activity and net contribution. Overall, in Asia and the Pacific, the share of the population aged 65 and above is projected to almost double between 2023 and 2050 from 10.1% to 17.1%, only leveling off toward the end of the century (Figure 2).

---

[8] In the People's Republic of China (PRC), from 3.1% in 2000 to 6.4% in 2030; in Georgia, from 5.7% in 2000 to 9.1% in 2030; and triple in Japan, from 4.7% in 2000 to 12% in 2030.

[9] International Labour Organization (ILO). 2018. *Care Work and Care Jobs for the Future of Decent Work.* https://www.ilo.org/wcmsp5/groups/public/---dgreports/---dcomm/---publ/documents/publication/wcms_633135.pdf.

[10] Some of the costs could be offset by an increase in tax revenue from the additional earnings and employment. ILO. 2022. *Care at work: Investing in care leave and services for a more gender equal world of work.* https://www.ilo.org/publications/major-publications/care-work-investing-care-leave-and-services-more-gender-equal-world-work

[11] For a population of around 72 million (2022). World Bank. 16 April. Population, total - Thailand. https://data.worldbank.org/indicator/SP.POP.TOTL?locations=TH.

[12] Lien Foundation. 2018. *Long Term Care Manpower Study.* http://www.lienfoundation.org/sites/default/files/Long%20Term%20Care%20Manpower%20Study%20FINAL_0.pdf.

[13] In the PRC, India, and the Republic of Korea, women spend nearly the equivalent of full-time working hours (40 hours) on childcare; PRC 31.9 hours; India 33.2 hours; and the Republic of Korea 34.1 hours.

[14] M. Boniol et al. 2022. The global health workforce stock and distribution in 2020 and 2030: a threat to equity and 'universal' health coverage? *BMJ Global Health* 7 (6). p. e009316. https://gh.bmj.com/content/bmjgh/7/6/e009316.full.pdf.

[15] Intergenerational living means households with both a member under age 20 years and a member aged 65 years and above. UN Department of Economic and Social Affairs. 2019. Patterns and trends in household size and composition: Evidence from a United Nations dataset. https://www.un.org/development/desa/pd/sites/www.un.org.development.desa.pd/files/agingtheme_household_size_and_composition_technical_report.pdf

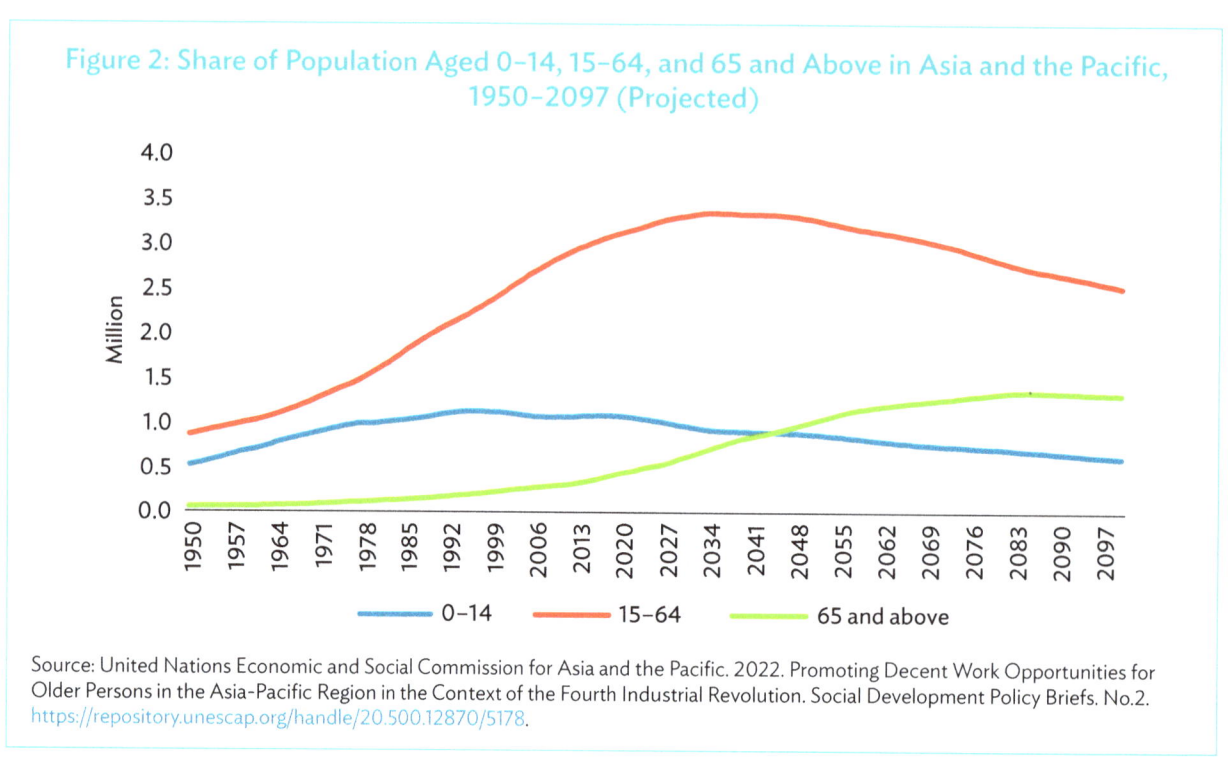

Figure 2: Share of Population Aged 0–14, 15–64, and 65 and Above in Asia and the Pacific, 1950–2097 (Projected)

Source: United Nations Economic and Social Commission for Asia and the Pacific. 2022. Promoting Decent Work Opportunities for Older Persons in the Asia-Pacific Region in the Context of the Fourth Industrial Revolution. Social Development Policy Briefs. No.2. https://repository.unescap.org/handle/20.500.12870/5178.

An aging workforce reduces productivity. Productivity over the working life cycle is in an inverted-U shape. Despite older workers having accumulated more experience, labor productivity is lowest for younger and older workers. As the median age of the labor force shifts upward, at some point average productivity begins to decline: *"Many empirical studies have found that GDP growth slows roughly one to one with declines in labor force and population growth."*[16] Demographic drag is greater in emerging than in advanced economies, i.e., labor productivity growth slows down with aging.[17] This implies a need for flexible, less-demanding jobs for older workers.

A large working-age population results in the highest demographic dividend—and job creation potential. If the workforce is relatively older with a decline in new entrants, two distinct effects on growth and productivity result. Output will decline if there are fewer workers (i.e., a decline in the working-age population, as has occurred, for example, in Japan) not offset by an increase in productivity, and output per capita will decline as the age composition of the labor force becomes older and less productive. Table 1 shows the diversity of demographic trends across countries in the Association of Southeast Asian Nations (ASEAN)+6 region. These countries are mainly aged or are aging rapidly with shrinking working-age shares. The early-dividend countries that are not yet "aged" (in terms of their share of population age 65 and above) and have declining fertility rates have potential for economic payoff. Households with lower numbers of children generally invest more per child, have more freedom for women to enter the formal workforce, and more household savings for old age.

---

[16] R. Lee and A. Mason. 2017. Cost of aging. *Finance & Development*. 54 (1). pp. 7–9. https://www.imf.org/external/pubs/ft/fandd/2017/03/pdf/lee.pdf.

[17] A. F. Gravina and M. Lanzafame. 2023. Demography, Growth, and Robots in Advanced and Emerging Economies. *ADB Economics Working Paper Series*. No. 701. ADB. https://www.adb.org/sites/default/files/publication/922246/ewp-701-demography-growth-robots.pdf.

Table 1: Demographic Trends in Association of Southeast Asian Nations+6 Countries

Country	Year that population share aged 65+ reached 7%	Year that population share aged 65+ reached 14%	Number of years between 7% and 14% share (actual or projected)	Aging status (as of 2023)	Demographic grouping (2015–2030 period)
Japan	1966	1993	27	Hyper-aged	Post-dividend
Australia	1950	2010	60	Aged	Post-dividend
New Zealand	1950	2012	62	Aged	Post-dividend
Singapore	2001	2021	20	Aged	Post-dividend
People's Republic of China	1998	2022	24	Aged	Late-dividend
Thailand	2002	2020	18	Aged	Late-dividend
Viet Nam	2011	2034	23 p	Soon aged	Late-dividend
Malaysia	2018	2042	24 p	Soon aged	Late-dividend
India	2020	2047	27 p	Soon aged	Early-dividend
Myanmar	2021	2050	29 p	Soon aged	Early-dividend
Indonesia	2019	2045	26 p	Soon aged	Early-dividend
Brunei Darussalam	2023	2037p	14 p	Not yet aged	Late-dividend
Cambodia	2025 p	2052 p	27 p	Not yet aged	Early-dividend

ASEAN+6 = 10 Association of Southeast Asian Nations (ASEAN) economies plus Australia, the People's Republic of China, India, Japan, the Republic of Korea, and New Zealand; p = projection.

Note: Aging status is determined as follows: "hyper-aged"—share of population aged 65+ is 20% or more; "aged"—share of population aged 65+ is more than 14% and less than 20%; "soon aged"—share of population aged 65+ is more than 7% and less than 14%; "not yet aged"—share of population aged 65+ is less than 7%. The categorization of demographic transition follows the World Bank definition. Post-dividend = total fertility rate in 1985 below 2.1 and shrinking working-age population share, 2015–2030; late-dividend = total fertility rate in 1985 above 2.1 and shrinking working-age population, 2015–2030; early-dividend = total fertility rate below 4 in 1985 and increasing working-age population share, 2015–2030; and pre-dividend = total fertility rate above 4 in 1985 and increasing working-age population share, 2015–2030.

Source: UNESCAP Demographic Changes in Asia and the Pacific: Country Profiles. https://www.population-trends-asiapacific.org/data; and S. Amer Ahmed. 2016. World Bank. 2016. Demographic Change and Development: A Global Typology. Policy Research Working Paper. 7893. World Bank Group. https://documents1.worldbank.org/curated/en/867951479745020851/pdf/WPS7893.pdf.

Labor Demand and Digital Transition

In many Asian economies, digitalization is contributing a growing share of GDP. These include Malaysia, Thailand, and Singapore. Five of the world's top economies in the information and communication technology (ICT) share of total patents are in Asia, signaling potential for innovation-driven growth.[18] Yet, the pace of change is highly variable across the region through the uneven diffusion of the infrastructure, knowledge base, and usage of digital technologies. Minimal participation in the digital economy requires being online. "Meaningful connectivity" requires some digital competencies, including knowledge of digital tools.[19] Mobile internet is fast becoming the most important means to bridge the region's digital divide. According to the Global System for Mobile Communications Association or GSMA, East Asia and Pacific has the highest mobile internet adoption rate after North America, Europe, and Central Asia at 71% usage, a more than 30% increase since 2017 (in 2022) (Figure 3).

---

[18] T. S. Sedik. 2018. Asia's Digital Revolution. Finance & Development Magazine. IMF. https://www.imf.org/en/Publications/fandd/issues/2018/09/asia-digital-revolution-sedik.

[19] International Telecommunication Union. *About UMC*. https://www.itu.int/itu-d/sites/projectumc/home/aboutumc/.

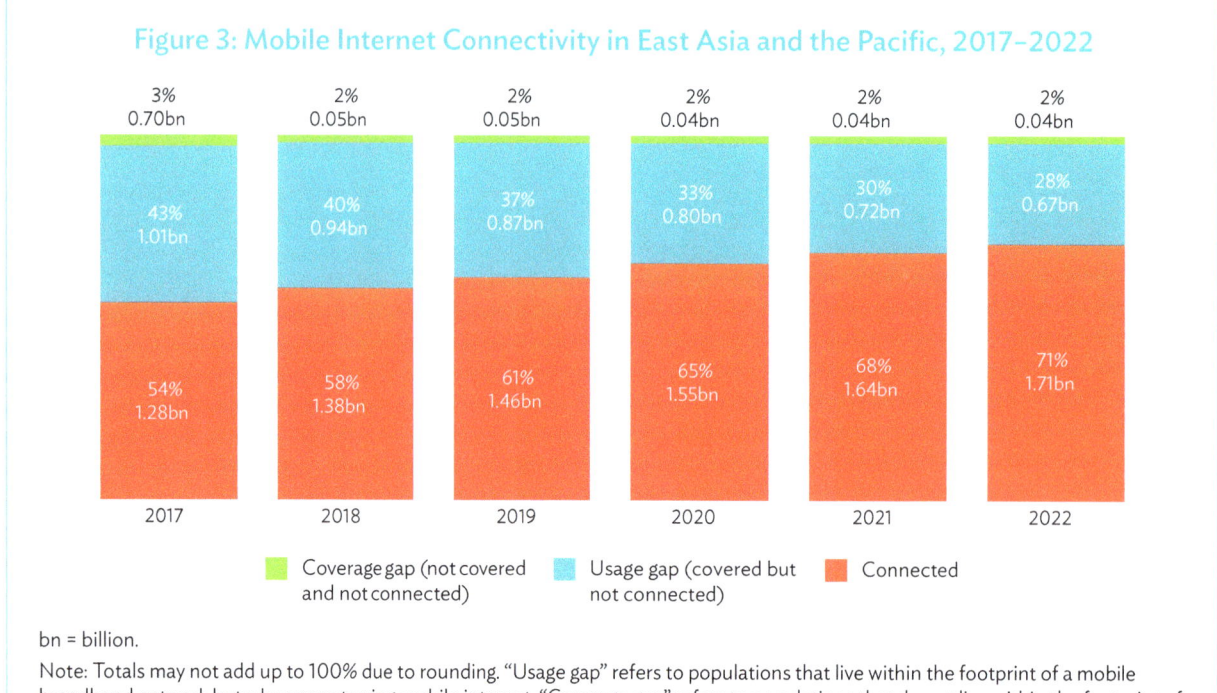

Figure 3: Mobile Internet Connectivity in East Asia and the Pacific, 2017–2022

bn = billion.
Note: Totals may not add up to 100% due to rounding. "Usage gap" refers to populations that live within the footprint of a mobile broadband network but who are not using mobile internet. "Coverage gap" refers to populations that do not live within the footprint of a mobile broadband network (3G or above).
Source: Global System for Mobile Communications Association (GSMA). 2023. The State of Mobile Internet Connectivity 2023. East Asia & Pacific Key Trends. https://www.gsma.com/r/wp-content/uploads/2023/10/State-of-Mobile-Internet-Connectivity-2023-East-Asia-and-Pacific.pdf.

The digital transition is profoundly transforming labor markets. First, digitalization both *creates* new sectors, occupations, and tasks (job creation), and *eliminates* redundant ones (job substitution). It also *augments* specific tasks of existing jobs, enhancing their performance, regardless of sector/industry or occupation (job complementing). These effects on jobs are dynamic. New ICT-intensive jobs (see Box 3 for definitions of digital jobs) can be created as digital technologies advance, but then become redundant as technologies continue to evolve. For example, data entry and analysis roles are being superseded by AI. Generative AI is having particularly transformative effects on jobs, due to its interplay with "human" cognitive capabilities.

Second, digitalization is changing the ways in which people engage with employment through more digital-dependent jobs. "Gig" work mediated via digital platforms collapses barriers to entry to the labor market, particularly those of time, place, and cost.[20] This eases labor force participation and can thus enable employment. Finally, a digitally networked economy implies a major reduction in transaction costs, eliminating barriers of time and distance, leading to a more efficient intermediation between labor supply and demand, boosting productivity. A 1-percentage-point increase in the digitalization of the People's Republic of China's (PRC) economy is associated with a 0.3-percentage-point in GDP growth (footnote 18).

---

[20] A digital platform is defined by the ILO as "a set of digital resources, including services and content that enable value-creating interactions between consumers and individual service-providing workers." Asia and the Pacific dominates developing regions in the prevalence and growth of platform work (Datta et al., 2023).

> **Box 3: Definitions of Digital Jobs**
>
> *ICT-intensive* jobs are those jobs in the information and communication technology (ICT) sector itself, such as programmers, software developers, and AI engineers.
>
> *ICT-dependent* jobs are jobs performed on digital platforms, such as Uber drivers, Upwork or Deliveroo workers, or freelance consultants.
>
> *ICT-enabled* jobs are those that are assisted by digital technologies but can be performed (less well) without it, such as accountants, surgeons, or graphic designers.
>
> Source: ILO, World Bank, and ADB.

A 2021 study by the Asian Development Bank (ADB) forecasted that in Asia and the Pacific, close to 65 million new jobs will be created yearly until 2025 from increased use of digital technologies. The digital sector in Asia would be worth $1.84 trillion by 2025, a rise of 31% from its value in 2020. Digital sector employment will rise by 7.1% in Central Asia, and in Southeast Asia by 6.2% in the same period.[21] Jobs such as AI and machine learning specialists, sustainability specialists, information security analysts, agricultural equipment operators, and database architects, among many others, are expected to be created.

Job impacts are sectoral. Agricultural equipment operators will see the highest job growth, creating more than 2.5 million jobs, while as many as 8–9 million data entry clerks will lose their jobs over the same period.[22] The labor-intensive ready-made garments sector in Bangladesh is experiencing net job loss: estimated in 2020 at a loss of 5.5 million jobs by 2041.[23] In Indonesia, ADB estimates that in the food and beverage sector, net job creation will be positive: 26% of the workforce could be displaced, but labor demand will increase by 41% due to Fourth Industrial Revolution effects. In the automotive manufacturing industry, the equivalent figures are 29% job loss and 30% job creation.[24]

Employment effects of automation depend on the relative costs of labor and capital. While 85% of construction jobs in Cambodia might be technically "at risk," it is unlikely that the risk would materialize if relative labor and capital costs continue to argue in favor of labor-intensive construction. This would not be the case in Japan, where the risk of automation is higher due to high labor costs and scarcity of labor supply.[25]

---

[21] ADB. 2021. *Asian Economic Integration Report 2021*. https://www.adb.org/sites/default/files/publication/674421/asian-economic-integration-report-2021.pdf.

[22] According to a survey by the World Economic Forum (WEF) of 803 companies—collectively employing more than 11.3 million workers—across 27 industry clusters and 45 economies from all world regions. The Future of Jobs Report 2023. https://www.weforum.org/reports/the-future-of-jobs-report-2023.

[23] UNDP. 2020. *Future of Work and SDG Attainment in the Age of Fourth Industrial Revolution—Bangladesh Perspective*. https://www.undp.org/bangladesh/stories/future-work-and-sdg-attainment-age-fourth-industrial-revolution%E2%80%94bangladesh-perspective.

[24] ADB. 2021. *Reaping the Benefits of Industry 4.0 Through Skills Development in Indonesia*. https://www.adb.org/sites/default/files/publication/671876/benefits-industry-skills-development-indonesia.pdf.

[25] D. Acemoglu and P. Restrepo. 2022. Demographics and automation. *The Review of Economic Studies*. 89 (1). pp. 1–44. https://doi.org/10.1093/restud/rdab031.

Technological disruptions lead to a reallocation of workers and jobs, i.e., greater structural labor market churn.[26] Churn is an important way to assess impacts of digital transition on jobs because even modest net change in the numbers of jobs can mask significant underlying reconfigurations and effects on workers. Jobs lost and those created will have different skill profiles and occur in different geographical locations, creating new dynamics for labor market inclusion. The World Economic Forum (WEF) finds that, globally, in the next 5 years, 152 million jobs will face a structural labor market churn. Across occupations, this represents 23% of current employment. Comparing data per economy in Asia and the Pacific included in the WEF sample, the churn rates range from 19% in Hong Kong, China to 30% in Pakistan. A 2017 McKinsey study projected that between 75 million and 375 million of the world's workers will need to switch occupational category by 2030, under different scenarios, equivalent to 14% of the global workforce.[27]

The latest digital advancements are affecting jobs differently compared to earlier stages of automation. Previous stages of automation (characterized by use of robotics and computerization, among other technologies) mainly displaced medium-skilled, routine jobs.[28] With the expansion of generative AI and large-language models, higher cognitive and nonroutine content is affected. Jobs that require nuanced judgment, creative problem-solving, or intricate data interpretation—traditionally the domain of highly skilled professionals—can now be augmented or even replaced by advanced AI algorithms, potentially exacerbating inequality across and within occupations:

> *"This shift challenges the conventional wisdom that technological advances threaten primarily lower-skilled jobs and points to a broader and deeper transformation of the labor market than by previous technological revolutions."*[29]

Of the world's jobs, 40% are exposed to AI-induced job changes (footnote 29). Estimates of job displacement vary depending on the estimation methodology, particularly whether an occupation- or a task-based approach is considered.[30] Automation mainly affects jobs in advanced economies, driven by the highest prevalence of high-skilled employment, faster adoption of AI, and existing high wages.[31] Wages are an important determinant of the job effects of labor-displacing technologies. Of Vietnamese garment industry workers, 86% are susceptible to displacement through automation, as wages in the sector rise.[32] However, in other garment-producing countries such as Bangladesh,

---

[26] Structural churn relates to the creation and destruction of roles, not the replacement of employees in the same role.

[27] Based on analysis in 46 economies accounting for around 90% of global GDP. Note that this study precedes the onset of generative AI. McKinsey and Company. 2017. *Jobs Lost, Jobs Gained: Workforce Transitions in a Time of Automation.* https://www.mckinsey.com/~/media/mckinsey/industries/public%20and%20social%20sector/our%20insights/what%20the%20future%20of%20work%20will%20mean%20for%20jobs%20skills%20and%20wages/mgi%20jobs%20lost-jobs%20gained_report_december%202017.pdf.

[28] Data on the skill composition of the labor force confirm the decline in the share of medium-skilled employment, and the increased share of high-skilled employment. The data do not suggest the disappearance of low-skilled labor, much of which may be nonroutine, and much of which is preponderant in locations to which the digital economy has not yet diffused in any case.

[29] M. Cazzaniga et al. 2024. Gen AI: Artificial intelligence and the future of work. *IMF Staff Discussion Note.* 14 January. p. 3. https://www.imf.org/en/Publications/Staff-Discussion-Notes/Issues/2024/01/14/Gen-AI-Artificial-Intelligence-and-the-Future-of-Work-542379.

[30] The task- and occupation-based approaches relate to whether displacement effects are analyzed at the task or job level, particularly whether the whole occupation (e.g., agricultural labor) could be displaced or only certain tasks/activities/functions (such as plowing) could be displaced.

[31] Microsoft. 2019. *Preparing for AI: The Implications of Artificial Intelligence for Jobs and Skills in Asian Economies.* https://news.microsoft.com/wp-content/uploads/prod/sites/43/2019/08/MS_Report_R2-1-pg-view-002.pdf.

[32] ILO. 2021. The Post-COVID-19 Garment Industry in Asia. ILO Research Brief. https://www.ilo.org/wcmsp5/groups/public/---asia/---ro-bangkok/documents/briefingnote/wcms_814510.pdf.

Cambodia, and India, relatively low wages of workers act as a disincentive for the entry of "sew-bots" into the industry. In Viet Nam—where the economy has outgrown its earlier dynamism based on the availability of low-cost, low-skilled labor—replacing labor by digital machinery such as sew-bots can renew the industry's competitiveness. In this scenario, job loss associated with partial automation reduces the extent of total job loss that would have occurred through relocation—a more nuanced (and more positive) net employment outcome than a mere jobs-at-risk assessment.

Technologies that result in job loss but also higher productivity and lower costs may lead to higher job-creating growth in a general equilibrium sense. Jobs lost to automation can result in increased productivity, thereby increasing competitiveness. This can increase job growth directly for the firm, and indirectly elsewhere in the firm's value chain through a multiplier effect. For example, in the Philippines, the IT-business process outsourcing sector will displace about one-quarter of jobs, but will simultaneously generate 34% of new jobs in upgraded services the sector will offer.[33] If production is more efficient, prices can go down, so disposable incomes can go up, which can raise aggregate demand, outweighing the negative impact of technology, leading to a net positive increase in employment.[34]

The future demand for labor cannot be fully known, as technologies continue to evolve and their full range of uses is a process of discovery. For example, digital technologies can "reinstate" tasks, "where a new technology increases the need for a wider array of labor-intensive tasks"[35]—an unforeseen outcome of unforeseen uses of technology. New jobs will be created that are not yet known. McKinsey used history as a guide to estimate that 8%–9% of 2030 labor demand will be in new types of occupations that have not existed before.[36] Social acceptability of AI will play a role in determining its ultimate impacts; the extent to which humankind considers its use to be appropriate in different contexts, such as making legal judgments (footnote 29).

Digitalization is also transforming the way people engage with employment through gig work. Digital labor markets can lower barriers to entry, including for workers with only basic digital skills—but with digital connectivity. In some countries of the region, gig employment growth is estimated to be about 30% in recent years. Digital labor platforms have played a major role in transforming the (often algorithm-based) mediation between labor supply and demand. Typically, workers are hired informally on a self-employed basis as independent contractors to complete short-term tasks or projects ("gigs"). Working methods, location of work, nature of work demanded by workers, and employer–employee relationships are reorganized, compared against standard forms of employment involving fixed duration of working hours, requirement of being physically present at the location of work, and labor laws governed by regulation. Platform workers are divided into those who deliver an immaterial or

---

[33] ADB. 2021. *Reaping the Benefits of Industry Through Skills Development in the Philippines.* https://www.adb.org/sites/default/files/publication/671881/benefits-industry-skills-development-philippines.pdf.

[34] ADB. 2018. *Asian Development Outlook (ADO) 2018: How Technology Affects Jobs.* https://www.adb.org/sites/default/files/publication/411666/ado2018.pdf.

[35] D. Acemoglu and P. Restrepo. 2018. The race between man and machine: implications of technology for growth, factor shares, and employment. *American Economic Review.* 108 (6). pp. 1488–1542. D. Acemoglu and P. Restrepo. 2019. Automation and new tasks: how technology displaces and reinstates labor. *Journal of Economic Perspectives.* 33 (2). pp. 3–30.

[36] McKinsey Global Institute. 2017. *Jobs Lost, Jobs Gained: Workforce Transitions in a Time of Automation.* https://www.mckinsey.com/~/media/mckinsey/industries/public%20and%20social%20sector/our%20insights/what%20the%20future%20of%20work%20will%20mean%20for%20jobs%20skills%20and%20wages/mgi%20jobs%20lost-jobs%20gained_report_december%202017.pdf.

"digital" product through an online exchange, and those who deliver "in situ" a material good or service, such as food delivery or rental accommodation. As ADB research finds:

> *"Usually, asymmetric information is the cause of high delivery costs and low access, and digital technology can bridge this information gap."*[37]

The past decade has seen a fivefold increase in the number of digital labor platforms globally, particularly in web-based and location-based platforms. The number of taxi and delivery platforms (i.e., location-based platforms) alone has grown tenfold during the period.[38] The ride-sharing economy in Bangladesh is valued at $259 million, 23% of the entire transportation sector in the nation, and is expected to grow further.[39] Of the world's workers, 12% are engaged in online gig work.[40] Three-quarters of platforms are regional or local, not global. East Asia and the Pacific is the third-highest subregion globally for location of platform headquarters (15%), after North America (39%) and the European Union (22%). Demand for online gig workers is rising faster in developing countries than in industrialized countries. Asia accounts for about 50% of digital platform revenue.

Gig work is generally performed by young people (aged 35 years or below). The average age of workers ranges from 27 years in India and the PRC, to 35 years in Indonesia, varying across services. For example, in India gig workers in the delivery services are relatively younger (average 27 years) compared with taxi services (33 years). Globally, over half of online gig workers are youth. Gig workers are motivated to join the platforms to earn extra income and work flexibly (Box 4). Flexibility can be particularly beneficial to female labor market inclusion. Working from home tends to be more important for women (35%) than men (25%), both in developing and developed countries. While women remain underrepresented, they are starting to participate to a greater extent in the online gig economy than in the general workforce in similar occupations. Six in 10 online gig workers live in smaller cities.[41]

---

[37] ADB Asian Economic Integration Report, Footnote 21, p. 187.
[38] ILO. 2021. *World Employment and Social Outlook: The role of digital labour platforms in transforming the world of work.* https://www.ilo.org/wcmsp5/groups/public/---dgreports/---dcomm/---publ/documents/publication/wcms_771749.pdf.
[39] Fairwork. 2021. *Fairwork Bangladesh Ratings 2021: Labour Standards in the Gig Economy.* https://fair.work/wp-content/uploads/sites/17/2021/12/Fairwork-Bangladesh-Report-2021-accessible-1.pdf
[40] Online gig work includes online freelancing and online microwork performed and delivered online, regardless of location.
[41] World Bank. 2023. *Working Without Borders: The Promise and Peril of Online Gig Work.* https://openknowledge.worldbank.org/entities/publication/ebc4a7e2-85c6-467b-8713-e2d77e954c6c.

Box 4: Gig Work Preferences Among Youth and Employers in Three Asian Economies—Results of an ADB-Commissioned Survey

Noting that most gig workers are young, research in Bangladesh, Georgia, and Indonesia surveyed a sample of students about their views on gig work.[a] Awareness of working in the gig economy was surprisingly low in Bangladesh and Indonesia (36% and 39% of students reported being "not at all aware," respectively, compared with 17% in Georgia).

Of the youth who reported awareness of gig work, flexibility in working hours was a consistent motivator in all countries (reported by 56% in Bangladesh, 57% in Georgia, and 58% in Indonesia). Georgian students were particularly incentivized by gaining supplementary income (73%). Youth in Indonesia considered gig work to be a pathway to higher incomes (67%), and some three-quarters (74%) wanted to work in gig jobs after gaining some experience. Half of respondents in Bangladesh expressed preferences to work in gig jobs in addition to a full-time job (this was lower in Indonesia, 10%, and Georgia, 33%).

Separately, employers in selected industries were also surveyed about the extent of gig-based hiring in their firms by skill level, and future plans.[b] Results varied by industry:

Indonesia:

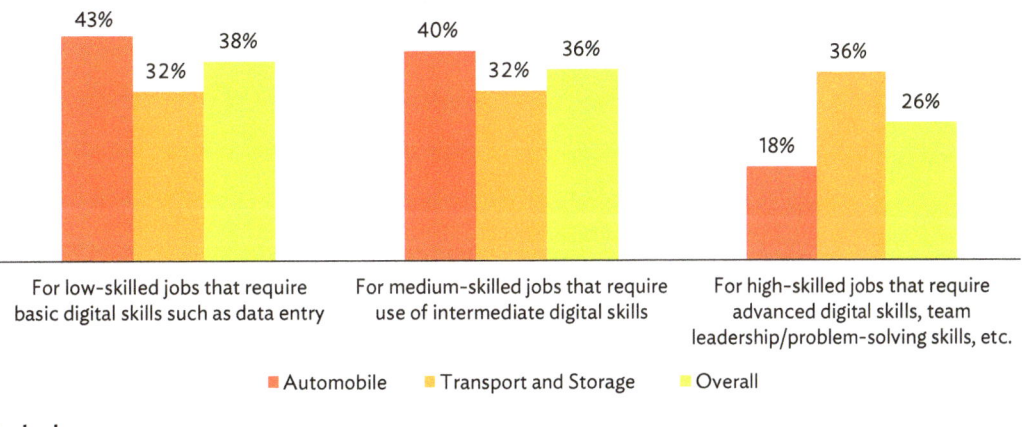

Bangladesh:

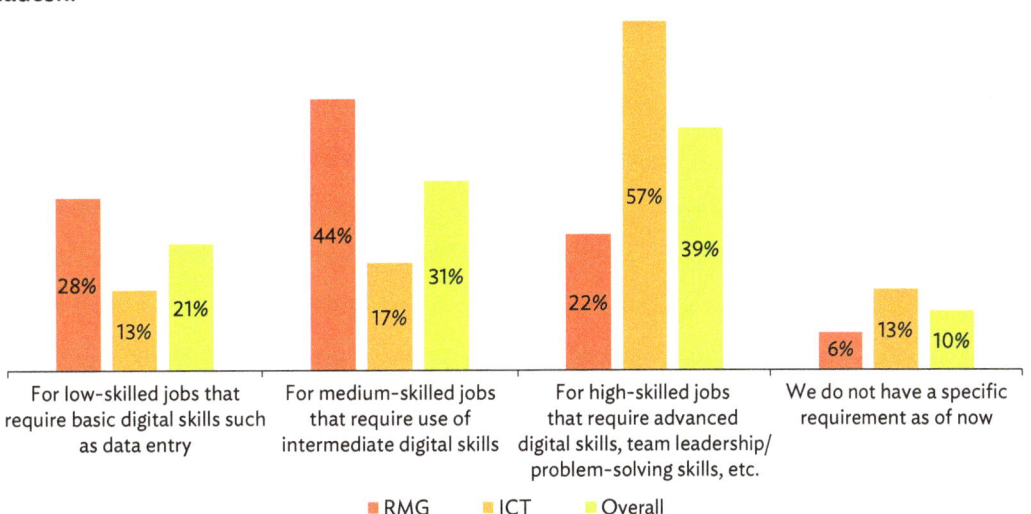

continued on next page

Box 4 continued

Georgia:

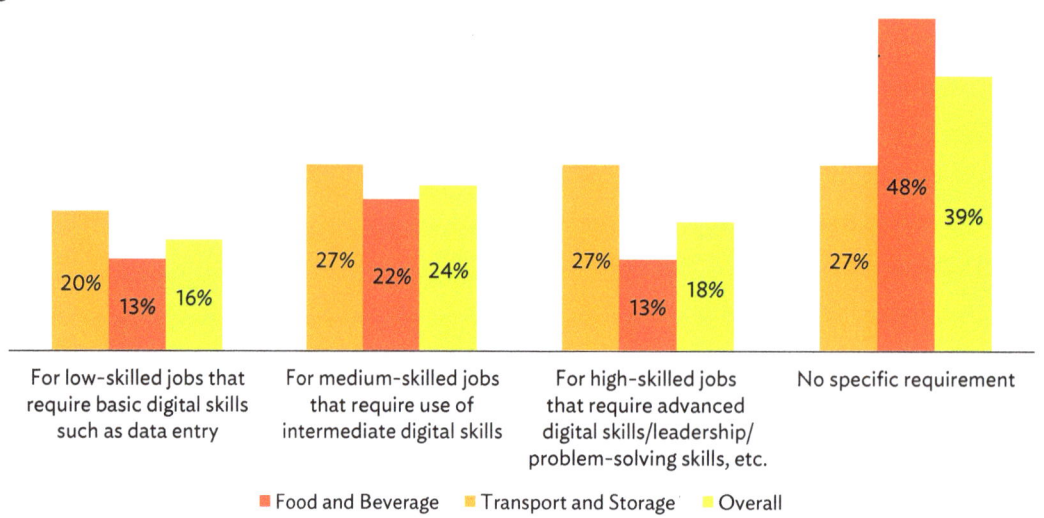

- Food and Beverage
- Transport and Storage
- Overall

^a Surveys were commissioned by PwC under ADB technical assistance Quality Jobs and Future of Work (TA 6533) and surveyed 600 students per country from a selection of general education and technical and vocational education and training (TVET) institutes. This sample excludes young people outside of formal education.
^b Selected industries: Ready Made Garments and ICT (Bangladesh); Food and Beverage and Transport and Storage (Georgia); Automotive and Transport and Storage (Indonesia).
Source: ADB consultants' report, PwC.

Labor Demand and Green Transition

Asia and the Pacific is at the center of the climate crisis. The region is both highly exposed to threats from climate change and a large contributor to greenhouse gas (GHG) emissions. The region's geography, including its coastlines, low-lying territories with dense populations, and numerous small island states, makes it exceptionally prone to rising sea levels and extremes in weather conditions. Of the 10 countries worldwide most affected by extreme weather events between 2000 and 2019, six were in Asia. An estimated half of the population in the Pacific live within 10 kilometers of the coast.[42] As a global manufacturing hub, Asia is also a major contributor to climate change. Three of the seven top GHG emitters in 2020 were from Asia (the PRC, India, and Indonesia). The region's urban areas produce 70% of global GHG emissions, primarily in the PRC,[43] and 38% of global energy-related GHG emissions come from the region.[44] If emissions stay high, economic losses resulting from climate change will be significant across developing Asia. Figure 4 shows declines in GDP resulting from climate impacts under a high-emissions scenario on key sectors (energy and transport, forestry, and agriculture), labor productivity, river flooding, and sea level rises for two countries and two subregions, with India, for example, at risk of a 7.3% decline in GDP by 2040 and a 35% decline by 2100.

---

[42] M. Mycoo et al. 2022. Small Islands. In *Climate Change 2022: Impacts, Adaptation and Vulnerability. Contribution of Working Group II to the Sixth Assessment Report of the Intergovernmental Panel on Climate Change.* By H.O. Pörtner et al., eds. Cambridge University Press, pp. 2043–2121. https://www.ipcc.ch/report/ar6/wg2/downloads/report/IPCC_AR6_WGII_Chapter15.pdf.

[43] L.P. Low. *Now or Never to Rein in Emissions: Highlights from IPCC Third Report and Implications in Asia Pacific.* https://www.pwc.com/gx/en/about/pwc-asia-pacific/ipcc-third-report-perspectives-on-asia-pacific.html.

[44] Climate Watch: Data Explorer. https://www.climatewatchdata.org/data-explorer (accessed 9 February 2024).

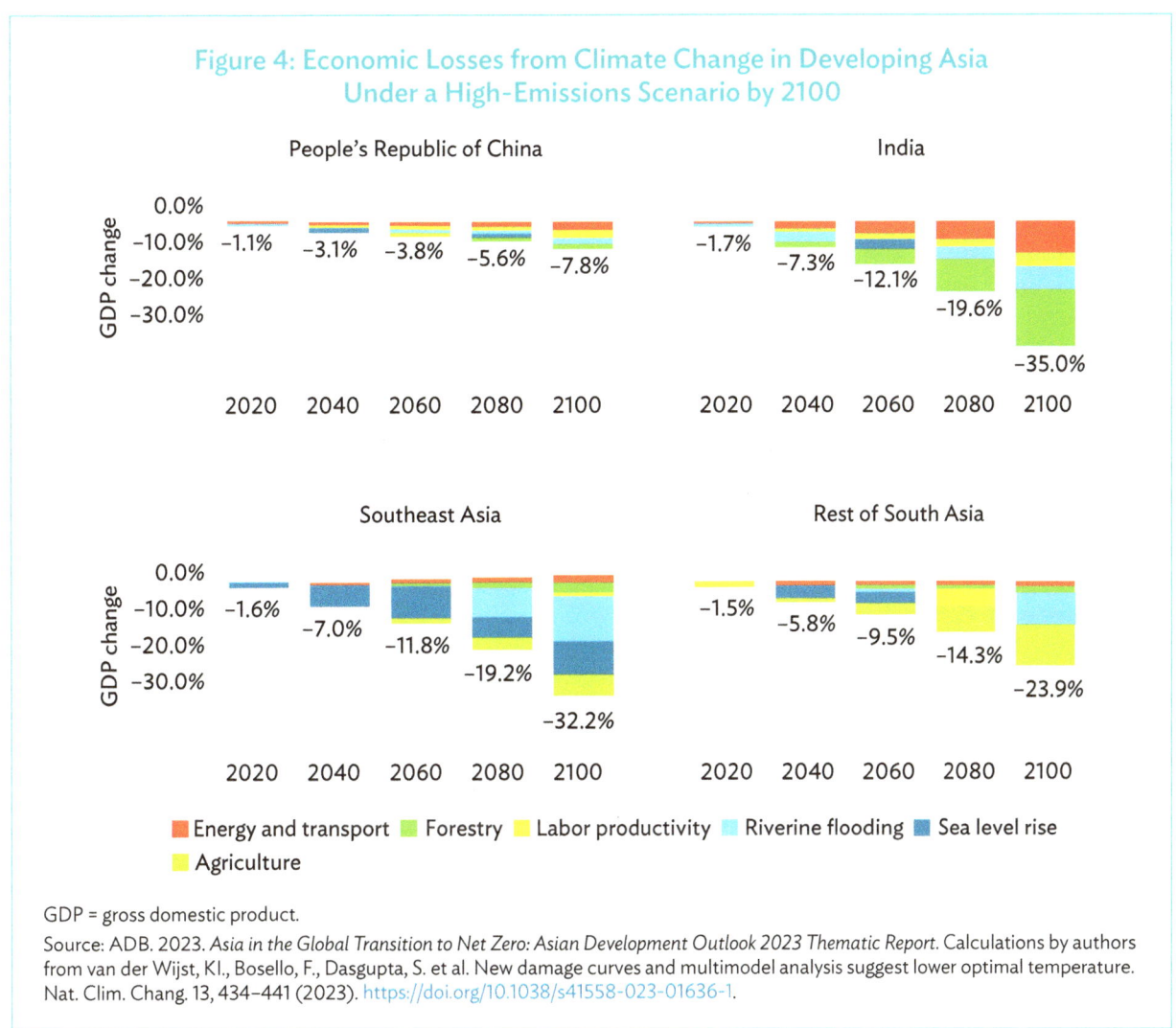

Figure 4: Economic Losses from Climate Change in Developing Asia Under a High-Emissions Scenario by 2100

GDP = gross domestic product.
Source: ADB. 2023. *Asia in the Global Transition to Net Zero: Asian Development Outlook 2023 Thematic Report*. Calculations by authors from van der Wijst, KI., Bosello, F., Dasgupta, S. et al. New damage curves and multimodel analysis suggest lower optimal temperature. Nat. Clim. Chang. 13, 434–441 (2023). https://doi.org/10.1038/s41558-023-01636-1.

Like the other two transitions, the green transition at once creates, substitutes, and alters jobs. The shift in economic activity out of high-carbon industries and processes into low-carbon alternatives results in the decline of polluting sectors and occupations and the emergence of more sustainable industries, jobs, and tasks. Industries (and jobs and tasks) that are major contributors to climate change are phased out in favor of more sustainable industrial approaches.[45] Decoupling the use of natural resources from economic growth can increase direct net employment in green sectors.[46] Shifting toward more energy-efficient production and consumption also changes the ways in which people

---

[45] The energy sector is a major focus, with its high carbon output transferred downstream as an input to a variety of manufacturing and service industries and consumption goods, such as automobiles. Agriculture and forestry, or land use, is a significant source of GHG (carbon dioxide and methane) emissions through deforestation that reduces the capture of carbon dioxide or "carbon sink" function of vegetation. Similarly, the built economy, i.e., construction and housing; and waste and water management. AusAID and ILO. Factsheet: Green Jobs in Nepal. https://www.ilo.org/sites/default/files/wcmsp5/groups/public/@asia/@ro-bangkok/@ilo-kathmandu/documents/projectdocumentation/wcms_160269.pdf.

[46] R. Maclean, S. Jagannathan, and B. Panth. 2018. *Education and Skills* for Inclusive Growth, Green Jobs and the Greening of Economies in Asia. ADB. https://www.adb.org/sites/default/files/publication/385041/education-skills-green-jobs.pdf.

work. A "greening" of economic activity applies across sectors, like digitalization. Over time, most jobs will evolve to accommodate sustainable practices and processes. Finally, climatic trends of warming alter conditions at work, and climatic shocks destroy and disrupt livelihoods, especially in the most exposed areas. Box 5 shows different definitions of green jobs.

Box 5: Definitions of Green Jobs

International Monetary Fund (IMF): Under the IMF's definition, the environmental properties of jobs are multidimensional, involving the extent to which workers undertake tasks that improve environmental sustainability (*green intensity*) and the degree to which their work involves activities exacerbating pollution (*pollution intensity*), as well as the level of emissions generated per worker (*emissions intensity*).

United Nations (UN): UN's definition of a green job combines environmental as well as job quality: "contributes to preserving or restoring the quality of the environment while also meeting the criteria for decent work—adequate wages, safe conditions, workers' rights, social dialogue and social protection."[a]

Asian Development Bank (ADB): ADB defines four categories of green jobs: (i) Sustainability—jobs in which the work process can be made more sustainable; all jobs are green jobs; (ii) Green Industry—jobs affiliated with economic activities that are deemed green by virtue of contributing to reducing carbon emissions; (iii) Task Profile—jobs that are affected by the green transition either by an increase in demand or change in task profile; and (iv) Green Task—jobs that have a high green skills intensity.

Country example—Cambodia: the Cambodia Climate Change Strategic Plan defines a green job as "individuals engaging in employment activities that preserve and restore environmental quality and help reduce negative environmental impacts" (ASEAN).

[a] Definitions of green jobs aim to incorporate sustainability in both output and process.

Sources: UNEP and ILO. 2008. Green Jobs: *Towards Decent Work in a Sustainable, Low-Carbon World*. https://www.unep.org/resources/report/green-jobs-towards-sustainable-work-low-carbon-world; ILO. 2021. *Regional Study on Green Jobs Policy Readiness in ASEAN - Final Report*. ASEAN and ILO. https://asean.org/wp-content/uploads/2021/06/ASEAN-Regional-Green-Jobs-policy-readiness-Report-web.pdf; A. Tsironis. 2023. Preparing the Workforce for the Low-Carbon Economy: A Closer Look at Green Jobs and Green Skills. *ADB Briefs* No. 262. https://www.adb.org/sites/default/files/publication/916561/adb-brief-262-workforce-low-carbon-economy.pdf.

Job estimates are net positive for climate change mitigation scenarios. The International Labour Organization's (ILO) modeling (based on the International Energy Agency (IEA) 2°C scenario, which compares with a baseline 6°C scenario) estimates a net increase at around 14.2 million green jobs in Asia and the Pacific, 79% of the global increase (Figure 6).[47] Other analysis by ILO finds that decarbonization is expected to generate up to 24 million green jobs by 2030 globally, the majority in Asia, while some 6 million jobs are expected to be lost, particularly in carbon-intensive industries.[48] Through a comprehensive decarbonization transition, Deloitte estimates that the economies of Asia

---

[47] ILO. 2018. *World Employment Social Outlook 2018: Greening with Jobs*. https://webapps.ilo.org/weso-greening/documents/WESO_Greening_EN_web2.pdf

[48] ILO. 2021. *Regional Study on Green Jobs Policy Readiness in ASEAN*. https://asean.org/wp-content/uploads/2021/06/ASEAN-Regional-Green-Jobs-policy-readiness-Report-web.pdf.

and the Pacific can add $47 trillion of value by 2070 and create 180 million jobs by 2050.[49] ADB estimated the impact of a $172 billion, five-part green growth strategy that can generate 30 million jobs in Southeast Asia by 2030.[50]

Job impacts will vary by sector. They will depend on sector carbon intensity and climate exposure. Sectors that are particularly exposed to climatic conditions need attention. Deloitte's modeling estimates that 43% of the Asia and Pacific workforce are employed in climate-vulnerable industries (agriculture, conventional energy, heavy industry and manufacturing, transport, and construction) (footnote 49). In the Pacific, more than one-quarter of the workforce is employed in agriculture, forestry, and fishing alone (28.4% of total employment). This rises to 45% in the Lao People's Democratic Republic and Myanmar. Shifting to organic and sustainable practices will be especially relevant.[51] Jobs in all sectors will be affected by "greening," i.e., shifting economic activity toward environmentally sustainable production and other processes:

> *"It appears that many existing jobs (especially those such as plumbers, electricians, metal workers, and construction workers) will be transformed and redefined as day-to-day skills sets, work methods, and profiles are greened."*[52]

In the renewable energy sector, technologies are currently more labor-intensive than fossil-fuel technologies. If countries continue dependency on fossil fuels, it is feasible that energy sector jobs will decline by 500,000 by 2030, as a result of increasing labor productivity.[53] Renewable energy sector employment (direct and indirect) grew from 7.3 million globally in 2012 to 12.7 million in 2021, with the solar photovoltaic (4.3 million, 2021) and bioenergy (3.4 million, 2021) industries the top two employers. Employment in renewables is estimated to increase to 38 million people globally by 2030, and 43 million by 2050, based on IEA's 1.5°C pathway.[54] Almost two-thirds of renewable jobs are in Asia, with the PRC alone accounting for 42% of the global total. Between 2019 and 2022, clean energy jobs were the major driver of energy job growth, outweighing losses in fossil-fuel jobs in almost all countries worldwide (except the Russian Federation and some countries in North Africa). In India, Indonesia, and the Middle East, fossil-fuel employment increased. The PRC underwent the largest rebalancing over the 2019–2022 period, with clean energy jobs growing by 2 million and fossil-fuel-related jobs falling by 600,000.[55]

---

[49] Deloitte. 2023. *Work Toward Net Zero in Asia Pacific*. https://www.deloitte.com/global/en/issues/climate/asia-pacific/asia-pacific-work-toward-net-zero.html.

[50] The five green growth areas are (i) productive and regenerative agriculture, (ii) sustainable urban development and transport, (iii) clean energy transition, (iv) circular economy models, and (v) healthy and productive oceans. ADB. 2022. *Implementing a Green Recovery in Southeast Asia*. https://www.adb.org/sites/default/files/publication/793536/implementing-green-recovery-southeast-asia.pdf.

[51] ILO. 2019. *Green Jobs and a Just Transition for Climate Action in Asia and the Pacific*.

[52] C. Martinez-Fernandez, C. Hinojosa, and G. Miranda. 2010. Greening Jobs and Skills. Labour Market Implications of Addressing Climate Change. OECD. https://doi.org/10.1787/5kmbjgl8sd0r-en.

[53] The energy sector is the largest global contributor of greenhouse gases. IRENA. Renewable Energy Jobs: Status, Prospects & Policies - an IRENA Working Paper. https://www.irena.org/-/media/Files/IRENA/Agency/Publication/2012/Renewable_Energy_Jobs_abstract.pdf.

[54] IRENA and ILO. 2022. *Renewable Energy and Jobs: Annual Review 2022*. https://www.ilo.org/wcmsp5/groups/public/---dgreports/---dcomm/documents/publication/wcms_856649.pdf.

[55] Globally, the energy sector employs over 67 million people (2022), equivalent to around 2% of global employment. IEA. *World Energy Employment 2023*. https://iea.blob.core.windows.net/assets/ba1eab3e-8e4c-490c-9983-80601fa9d736/World_Energy_Employment_2023.pdf.

The redistributive job effects of the green transition are significant. Firms consider the green transition to be the most significant driver of job creation over the next 5 years.[56] The reshaping of labor markets will displace some workers and create new opportunities for others. There can be a temporal lag, with job losses preceding job gains. There is only a limited evidence base to measure the redistributive impacts on locations and workers, noting the potential for increased spatial and income inequalities.[57] People with lower levels of educational attainment and skills mainly work in polluting jobs, and are less likely to take part in traxining. Transitioning from a nongreen to a green job can be challenging. For workers in pollution-intensive work and in environmentally neutral work, the probability of transition into greener work is low (and not statistically significantly different) for both groups of workers.[58] In absolute terms, the job effects of green policy interventions—a shift of about 1% of employment into the lower-emissions-intensive sector over 10 years—are lower than the labor reallocation that took place from industrial to service sectors in the 1980s in many advanced economies (4% per decade) (footnote 58). The job effects of mitigation and adaptation strategies will depend on the design of interventions. Some will generate more jobs, others will reduce labor demand. For example, fisheries quotas will limit employment in the sector.[59]

Climate change is itself increasingly a determinant of economic opportunity. It intersects with processes of development, affecting capacity for productive work:

> "Climate change will become a more conspicuous economic driver in the coming decade as climate vulnerability intensifies in major portions of South and Southeast Asia" (IOM).[60]

If people are already vulnerable, the climate effects compound with other non-climatic stressors of vulnerability—including low levels of savings, poor health, or weak infrastructure—to disrupt livelihoods. Climate effects can be slow, such as sea level rise or ocean acidification, or sudden, such as floods or landslides, affecting livelihoods differently, for example, long-term crop degradation over time, or one-off crop wipe-out. Jobs most exposed to the natural world tend to be the occupations of the rural poor, notably agriculture, forestry, fisheries, but also the urban poor, especially in construction. While the quantification of livelihood risk is difficult to assess with any precision, agriculture remains the largest employment sector in the region.

It is estimated that rising temperatures can lead to a global loss of productivity equivalent to 80 million full-time jobs. Heat stress is a growing challenge for vulnerable workers (Figure 5). A 50% reduction in labor productivity is associated with temperatures at or above 33°C–34°C. Since adaptive capacity to climate change varies across the region, countries in South Asia and Southeast Asia are projected to be affected more than those in other subregions. Thailand, Cambodia, and India are

---

[56] World Economic Forum. The Future of Jobs Report 2023. https://www.weforum.org/publications/the-future-of-jobsreport-2023.

[57] Recent OECD modeling aims to show wide *in-country* variance in the losses and creation of green jobs. OECD. 2023. *Job Creation and Local Economic Development 2023: Bridging the Great Green Divide*. OECD Publishing. https://doi.org/10.1787/21db61c1-en.

[58] IMF. 2022. Ch 3 *World Economic Outlook: War Sets Back The Global Recovery*. The modeled policy package includes a green infrastructure push, carbon tax, targeted training program, and an earned income tax credit.

[59] ILO. 2019. *Green Jobs and a Just Transition for Climate Action in Asia and the Pacific*.

[60] International Organization for Migration. 2023.*Labour Migration in Asia: What Does the Future Hold?* https://publications.iom.int/books/labour-migration-asia-what-does-future-hold.

projected to lose close to 6% of their GDP, while Indonesia, Myanmar, and Papua New Guinea would lose less than 3%.[61]

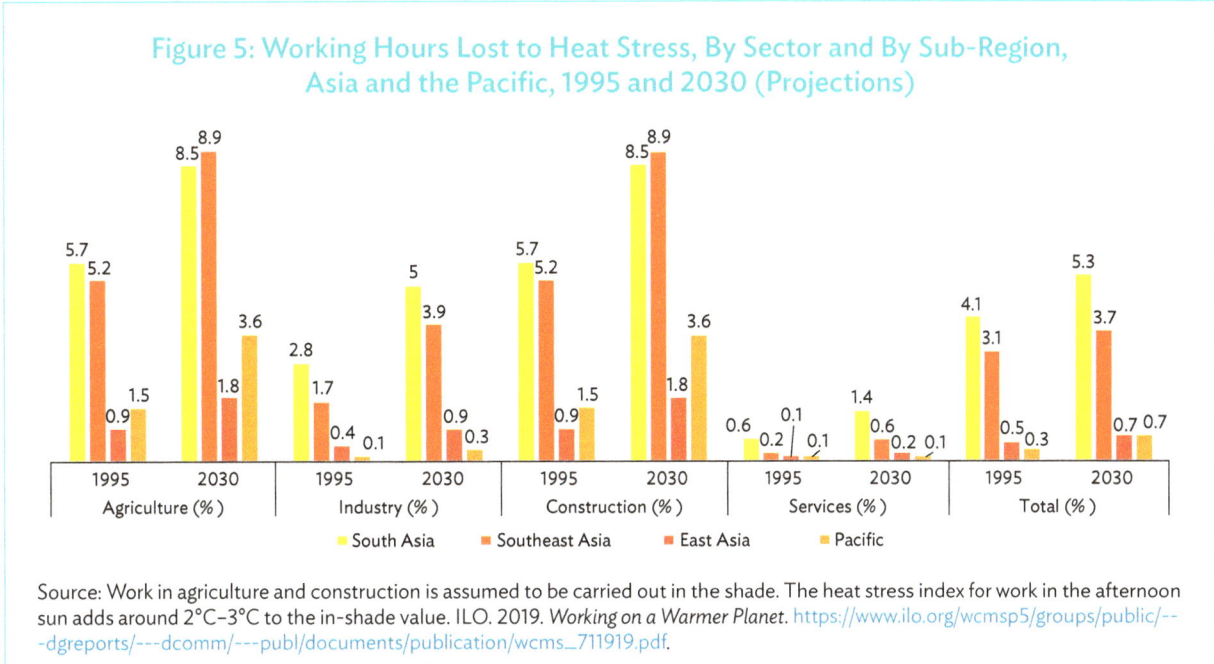

Figure 5: Working Hours Lost to Heat Stress, By Sector and By Sub-Region, Asia and the Pacific, 1995 and 2030 (Projections)

Source: Work in agriculture and construction is assumed to be carried out in the shade. The heat stress index for work in the afternoon sun adds around 2°C–3°C to the in-shade value. ILO. 2019. *Working on a Warmer Planet*. https://www.ilo.org/wcmsp5/groups/public/---dgreports/---dcomm/---publ/documents/publication/wcms_711919.pdf.

Job Quality and Skills

The effects of the triple transition on labor demand have implications for job quality. For the purpose of this study, job quality has been confined to two dimensions: skill endowment and social protection coverage. This provides a lens into informality in the triple transition, with vulnerable workers often in low-skilled, precarious, and unprotected work. Taking first skills, human capital is fundamental to unlocking the benefits of the triple transition. For workers, skills underpin wages and well-being. Higher-skilled jobs result in higher incomes.[62] For firms, matching skilled workers to labor demand drives productivity. Labor productivity depends on skills at the whole-economy level. Countries that can meet the demand for skills have been found to have lower wage inequality.[63]

---

[61] ILO. 2019. *Working on a Warmer Planet*. https://www.ilo.org/wcmsp5/groups/public/---dgreports/---dcomm/---publ/documents/publication/wcms_711919.pdf.

[62] It is recognized that a "quality" job necessitates a range of other features, in line with international standards, for example, related to stability and security of work. In the renewable energy sector, an important growth area, currently 60%–70% of jobs in India are informal. Indonesia, followed by the United States and Brazil—the dominant producers for biodiesel—hire large numbers of workers, often employed informally and seasonally. With 500,000 such workers in Indonesia, 180,000 in Colombia, 130,000 million in Thailand, 60,000 in Malaysia, and 30,000 in Philippines, Asia and the Pacific employs a significant number of "green" workers informally. These are important considerations for further exploration of the jobs potential of the triple transition.

[63] OECD. 2019. *OECD Employment Outlook 2019. The Future of Work*. Paris. https://www.oecd.org/en/publications/oecd-employment-outlook-2019_9ee00155-en.html.

The megatrends imply an upward skill bias in the demand for labor. The current skill composition of countries in the region is dominated by medium-skilled jobs. Skills in greatest demand in the medium-term future are a mix of technical skills—related to demand in the care, digital, and green economies—and soft skills. Table 2 provides an overview of known changes in the demand for skills resulting specifically from the three transitions. In particular, the nonroutine and cognitive nature of new jobs emphasizes the importance of higher-order cognitive and soft skills. Data from India, Indonesia, Thailand, and Viet Nam show that in those jobs that require nonroutine cognitive tasks, wages have grown faster over the past decade (footnote 34). Analysis in Viet Nam is particularly instructive: the wages in emerging occupations are higher than in established occupations, but levels of employment in emerging occupations is "very low." The job quality potential of new jobs is high, yet access and inclusion may be minimal due to the scarcity of new jobs.

Table 2: Overview of Changes to Demand for Skills Resulting from the Triple Transition

Transition 1: Demographic transition	
The likelihood of skill obsolescence increases relative to age, so aging populations can imply declining competitiveness. Equipping new labor market entrants with relevant skills helps to maintain the productivity equilibrium. Equally, upskilling older workers can lengthen their economic contribution. For example, in Japan, a rapidly aging economy, it is expected that by 2060, at least 70% of the elderly population (aged 50–64 years) will have postsecondary education, up from 40% in 2022.[a]	The expanding care economy calls for relevant skills to meet the demands of health care, wellness, social services, and community care across the age spectrum. The Singapore Government Agency, "MySkills Future" identified five skill clusters that feature prominently in the care economy: Conduct and Ethics, Stakeholder Management, Inclusive Practices, Reflective Practice, and Change Management Framework.[b] Upskilling can also enable pathways toward work with better-quality conditions.
Transition 2: Digital transition	
From basic to advanced, all digital skills are in demand in the digital economy, and become critical for labor market inclusion. About 70% of employers reported that basic and applied digital skills are now a "workplace essential" in Bangladesh, India, Indonesia, and the Philippines.[c]	In digital labor markets, it is increasingly the possession of skills, not qualifications, that matters. Digital skills are of increasing relevance to the economic value (at least) of education, with acquisition increasingly through alternative, nonformal education channels, such as boot camps. In emerging fields like cybersecurity and robotics, advanced skills are required, but not necessarily advanced degrees, in so-called "new collar" jobs.[d]
The large share of "digital-dependent" jobs in the digital economy all require basic digital literacy.	Skills that strengthen the human contribution of labor compared with technology will increasingly define digital work, i.e., "soft" skills of critical thinking, reasoning, self-reflection.

continued on next page

Table 2 continued

Transition 3: Green transition	
New skills associated with core green technologies will be at the medium or advanced skill level, both for existing and for incoming workers. Of new clean energy jobs, 60% will require postsecondary education.[e]	Adaptation ("greening") of existing skill sets appears to be the quantitatively greater skills agenda than the acquisition of entirely new skills focusing on core green technologies, such as renewable energy.
"Greening" of jobs spans all skill levels. The share of green talent in the agriculture sector has grown to become the highest sector share in the Asia and Pacific region. Dairy and farming subsectors, for example, have seen an increasingly high intensity of "green skills" in Australia. The share of green talent in Indian farming and dairy sectors has also grown at a compound annual growth rate of 6%.[f]	

[a] UNESCAP. 2023. *The Future of Work in the Context of Population Ageing in Asia and the Pacific.* https://www.unescap.org/kp/2023/future-work-context-population-ageing-asia-and-pacific.
[b] SkillsFuture Singapore. 2024. *The Care Economy Explained: Trends, Skills & Jobs You Need to Know About.* https://www.myskillsfuture.gov.sg/content/portal/en/career-resources/career-resources/job-skills-insights/the-care-economy-explained-trends-skills-jobs-you-need-to-know.html.
[c] ADB. 2022. *Digital Jobs And Digital Skills.* https://www.adb.org/sites/default/files/publication/829711/digital-jobs-digital-skills.pdf.
[d] L. Kelley. 2024. With 'New Collar' Jobs, Advanced Skills Stand Out. New York Times. 4 January. p.8.; C. Ammerman, B. Groysberg, and G. Romerty. 2023. The New-Collar Workforce. Harvard Business Review. March–April. https://hbr.org/2023/03/the-new-collar-workforce.
[e] International Energy Agency. 2022. World Energy Employment. https://iea.blob.core.windows.net/assets/a0432c97-14af-4fc7-b3bf-c409fb7e4ab8/WorldEnergyEmployment.pdf. Of employment in the energy sector, at least 45% of jobs in 2019 required highly skilled workers, and 50%, medium-skilled workers.
[f] LinkedIn Economic Graph. Global Skills Report 2022. https://economicgraph.linkedin.com/content/dam/me/economicgraph/en-us/global-green-skills-report/global-green-skills-report-pdf/li-green-economy-report-2022.pdf.

A skills shortage to adapt to changing labor demand creates a brake on the pace of the structural transformation. The transition to a digital, low-carbon, inclusive economy relies on both the skill composition of new entrants to the labor market, as well as the skills of existing workers and the institutional and enterprise facility with which re-skilling or upskilling is enabled. A skills gap in the region is well-documented.[64] The pace of change makes gaps inevitable. The need for upskilling is sizable and ongoing. For example, across seven economies of the region, some 86 million workers need training in digital skills in a year.[65] There is greater availability of skills for the digital transition in higher-income countries in the region (Figure 6). Even in countries leading ICT industry and digital advances, such as the PRC and India, there is a scarcity of human capital for the digital economy.[66]

---

[64] See among others: Economist Impact. 2023. *Bridging the skills gap: fuelling careers and the economy in Asia-Pacific.* The Economist Group. https://impact.economist.com/perspectives/sites/default/files/bridging_the_skills_gap_fuelling_careers_and_the_economy_in_asia_pacific.pdf.
[65] The seven countries are Australia, India, Indonesia, Japan, New Zealand, Singapore, and the Republic of Korea. AlphaBeta. 2022. *Building Digital Skills for the Changing Workforce in Asia Pacific And Japan (APJ).* March. https://cdn.accesspartnership.com/wp-content/uploads/2023/01/aws-apj-en-fa-onscn.pdf.
[66] Cisco Systems prepared a global ranking of 143 countries on the basis of the availability of adequate skilled human resources in the country to build and maintain digital systems and support digital innovation in the country. Singapore leads the global, not just regional league. The Human Capital Index is a composite comprising the literacy rate, educational attainment, internationally comparable test scores (e.g., PISA), and labor force participation. The two most populated countries, the PRC and India, noted worldwide for their ICT industry and digital advances, score rather low in overall human resource readiness.

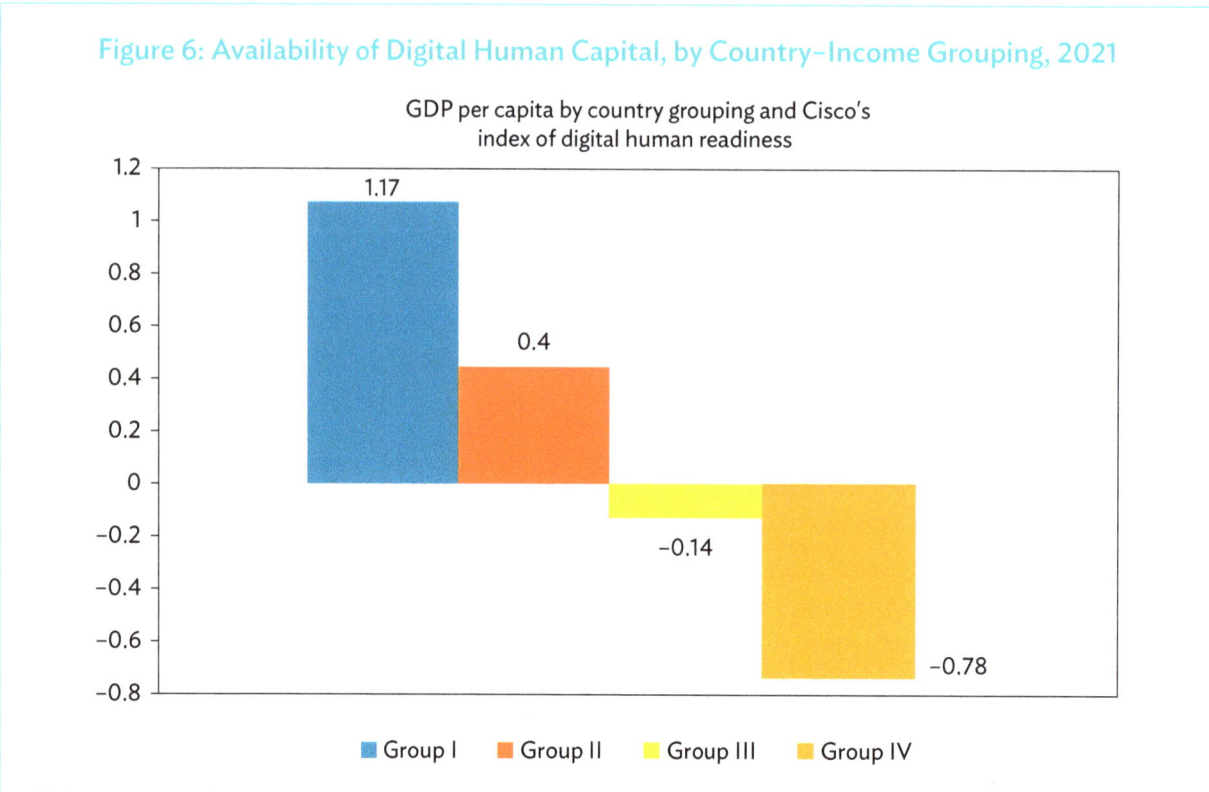

Figure 6: Availability of Digital Human Capital, by Country–Income Grouping, 2021

GDP = gross domestic product.

Note: The figure shows the average Human Capital indicator score matched to the average, logged GDP per capita for each of the four country quartiles. Each quartile has an equal number (seven) of countries grouped by GDP per capita from highest to lowest from a sample of 28 countries in the region: Group I is highest GDP per capita and Group IV is lowest.

Authors' groupings of countries by income group: Group I includes Singapore, Australia, New Zealand, Japan, the Republic of Korea, the PRC, and Malaysia; Group II includes Kazakhstan, Azerbaijan, Armenia, Thailand, Georgia, Mongolia, and Indonesia; Group III includes Viet Nam, the Philippines, Sri Lanka, India, Bangladesh, Uzbekistan, and the Lao People's Democratic Republic; Group IV includes Cambodia, Pakistan, the Kyrgyz Republic, Nepal, Myanmar, Tajikistan, and Afghanistan

Source: World Bank data for GDP per capita; Cisco Human Capital component of Digital Readiness Index. https://www.cisco.com/c/m/en_us/about/corporate-social-responsibility/research-resources/digital-readiness-index.html#/Human%20Capital.

A key issue in addressing the digital skills shortage is an "institutional bottleneck." A recent Organisation for Economic Co-operation and Development (OECD) survey found that the greatest skills shortage was in teachers and trainers equipped to impart relevant digital skills in demand by employers. In developing economies, skills acquisition is often impeded by outdated curricula and staff competencies among traditional vocational training institutions. ADB-commissioned research by PricewaterhouseCoopers (PwC) found major concerns among training institutes about the quality of teachers for courses related to the Fourth Industrial Revolution (Figure 7).[67]

---

[67] A sample of around one-third of general education and technical and vocational education and training institutes was selected.

Figure 7: Institutional Barriers to Fourth Industrial Revolution Training Delivery and Curricula Updating—Results of an ADB-Commissioned Survey in Bangladesh, Georgia, and Indonesia

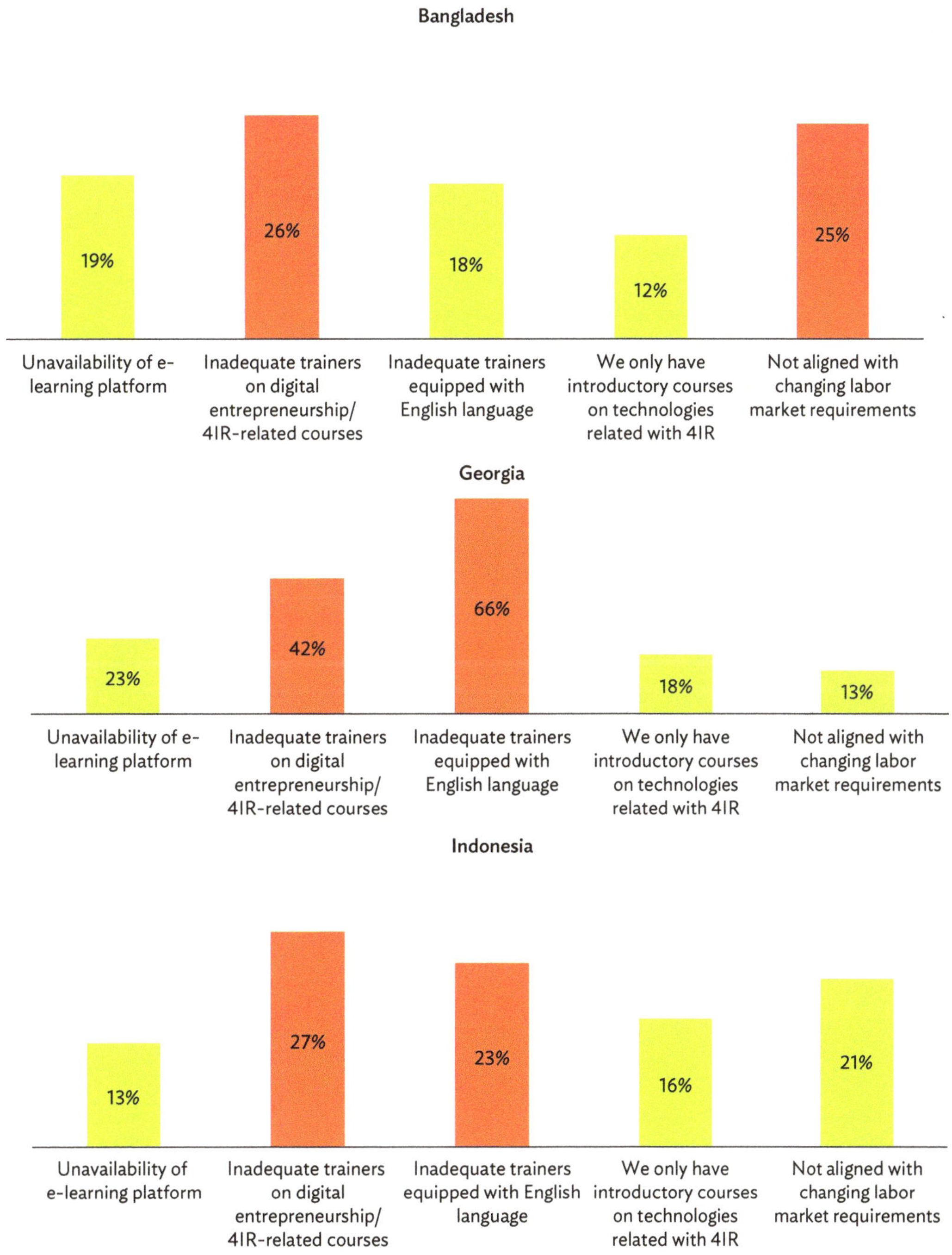

Bangladesh

Barrier	%
Unavailability of e-learning platform	19%
Inadequate trainers on digital entrepreneurship/4IR-related courses	26%
Inadequate trainers equipped with English language	18%
We only have introductory courses on technologies related with 4IR	12%
Not aligned with changing labor market requirements	25%

Georgia

Barrier	%
Unavailability of e-learning platform	23%
Inadequate trainers on digital entrepreneurship/4IR-related courses	42%
Inadequate trainers equipped with English language	66%
We only have introductory courses on technologies related with 4IR	18%
Not aligned with changing labor market requirements	13%

Indonesia

Barrier	%
Unavailability of e-learning platform	13%
Inadequate trainers on digital entrepreneurship/4IR-related courses	27%
Inadequate trainers equipped with English language	23%
We only have introductory courses on technologies related with 4IR	16%
Not aligned with changing labor market requirements	21%

4IR = Fourth Industrial Revolution.
Note: Responses show % of educational institutions facing challenges in updating their curricula. Bangladesh N = 121; Georgia N = 31; Indonesia N = 105.
Source: ADB consultants' report, PwC.

Skills play an important role in technology adoption, which can affect the pace of transformation through the triple transition. A technology-and-training combination leads to productivity gains in firms.[68] Lack of capabilities among workers is perceived by firms as a high barrier to adopt and use technology.[69] It is technological advancement that drives the productivity effects of environmental policies on firms and sectors. At the micro level, climate-smart digital tools for farmers can improve knowledge of weather and markets, and decrease time inefficiencies, leading to better yields and income generation—with induced effects on local consumption (FAO 2021).[70]

Skills required for work are constantly changing in line with shifting labor demand. Of existing "core skills" demanded by employers at the high end of the occupational spectrum of employees, 44% will change over the next 5 years (footnote 56). Such change means "learnability" becomes a core capability for work, understood as "the ability and willingness to learn to unlearn and relearn."[71] Learning shifts to become a mindset among workers and employers, rather than a task. Propensity for learning will evolve as a competitive differentiator among workers.

Job Structures and Social Protection

Social protection enables economic change to occur. Social protection spending is correlated with increased labor productivity (Figure 8). Providing resilience speeds a return to growth from socioeconomic shock or structural disruption and at lower social cost.[72] As shown in the previous section, labor market churn rates will increase in the triple transition. New categories of labor market "winners and losers" will emerge through job creation, substitution, and disruption. As a consequence, demands on social protection systems will rise. Through social assistance, insurance, and activation policies, people will variously need appropriate support to manage smooth transitions into, through, and out of a changing labor market. Demand for social protection is being transformed by megatrends. This has implications for job quality, with the extent and nature of coverage determining precarity among workers in the triple transition.

---

[68] D. Boothby, A. Dufour, and J. Tang. 2010. Technology adoption, training and productivity performance. *Research Policy* 39 (5). pp. 650-661. https://www.sciencedirect.com/science/article/pii/S0048733310000594.

[69] See for example a survey of firms in Viet Nam. Capabilities refer to both lack of information on what technologies are available and also lack of skills to use the technology. X. Cirera et al. 2021. Firm-Level Technology Adoption in Vietnam. *Policy Research Working Paper* 9567. World Bank Group. https://documents1.worldbank.org/curated/en/498501615216149075/pdf/Firm-Level-Technology-Adoption-in-Vietnam.pdf.

[70] Food and Agriculture Organization of the United Nations (FAO). 2021. Climate-smart agriculture case studies 2021 – Projects from around the world. https://doi.org/10.4060/cb5359en.

[71] S. Ra et al. 2019. The rise of technology and impact on skills. *International Journal of Training Research*. 17 (sup1). pp. 26–40. https://www.tandfonline.com/doi/full/10.1080/14480220.2019.1629727

[72] The standard deviation on social protection spending as a share of GDP is greater with a lower level of national income.

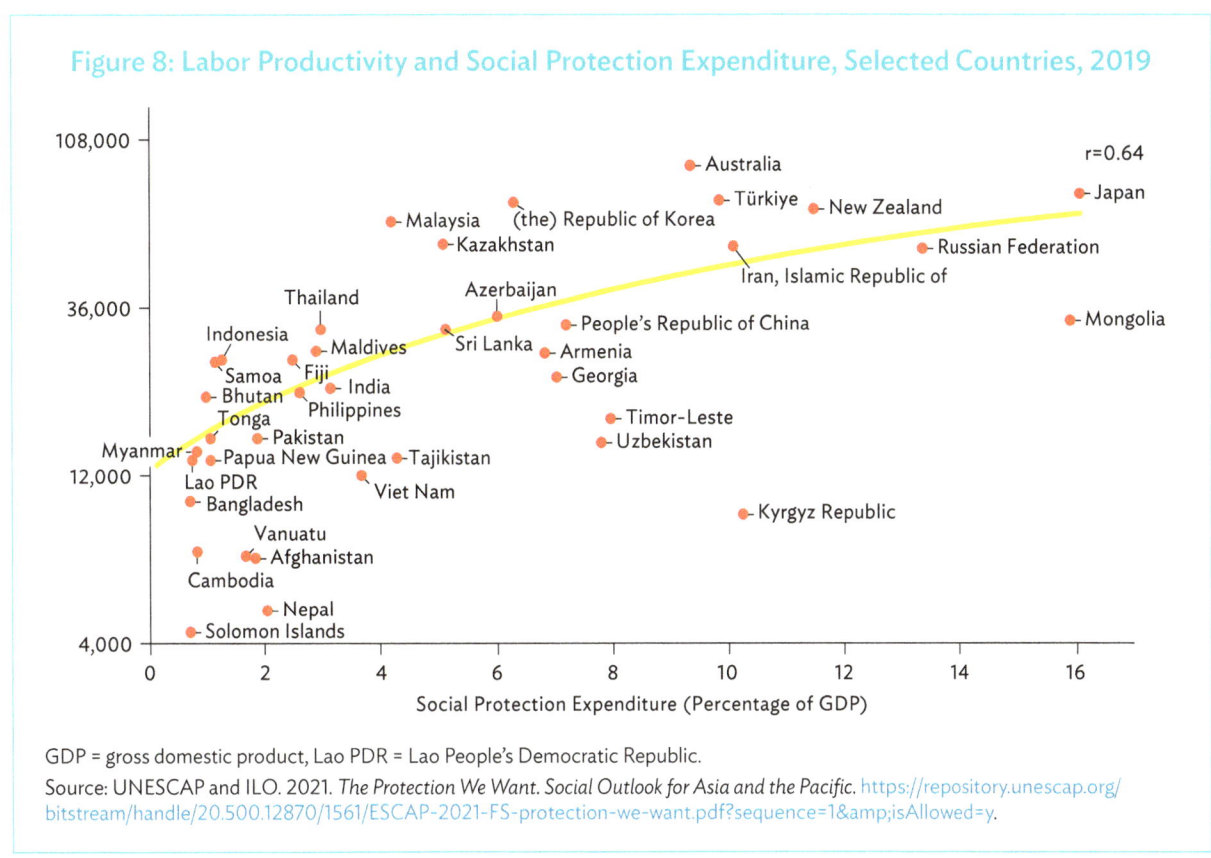

GDP = gross domestic product, Lao PDR = Lao People's Democratic Republic.
Source: UNESCAP and ILO. 2021. *The Protection We Want. Social Outlook for Asia and the Pacific*. https://repository.unescap.org/bitstream/handle/20.500.12870/1561/ESCAP-2021-FS-protection-we-want.pdf?sequence=1&isAllowed=y.

The demographic transition is challenging the solvency of social protection systems. A decline in new entrants to the labor force in the context of increasing longevity—a decline, therefore, in the relative size of the working-age population—depletes the resources of contributory-based pension systems. Globally, the dependency ratio is projected to shift from four working people for every one retired in 2023, to two working people to every four retired in 2050.[73] At the same time, the share of older people working beyond the traditional upper limit of 65 years is often substantial (Figure 9). The labor force participation rate among men aged 65+ is 32% in developing Asia (compared with an average OECD rate of 20.7%) and 15.3% for women aged 65+ (11.1% OECD average). This can reflect the absence or inadequacy of old-age pensions. In the region, 94% of workers aged 65+ are working informally, often excluded from social protection coverage.[74]

---

[73] Sydney Business Insights. Demographic Change. https://sbi.sydney.edu.au/megatrends/demographic-change/.
[74] UNFPA. COVID-19 and older people in Asia Pacific: 2020 (in review). https://socialprotection.org/sites/default/files/publications_files/covid19-and-older-people-in-asia-pacific-2020-in-review.pdf; ADB. 2024. *Aging Well in Asia: Asian Development Policy Report*. https://www.adb.org/sites/default/files/publication/964571/asian-development-policy-report-2024.pdf.

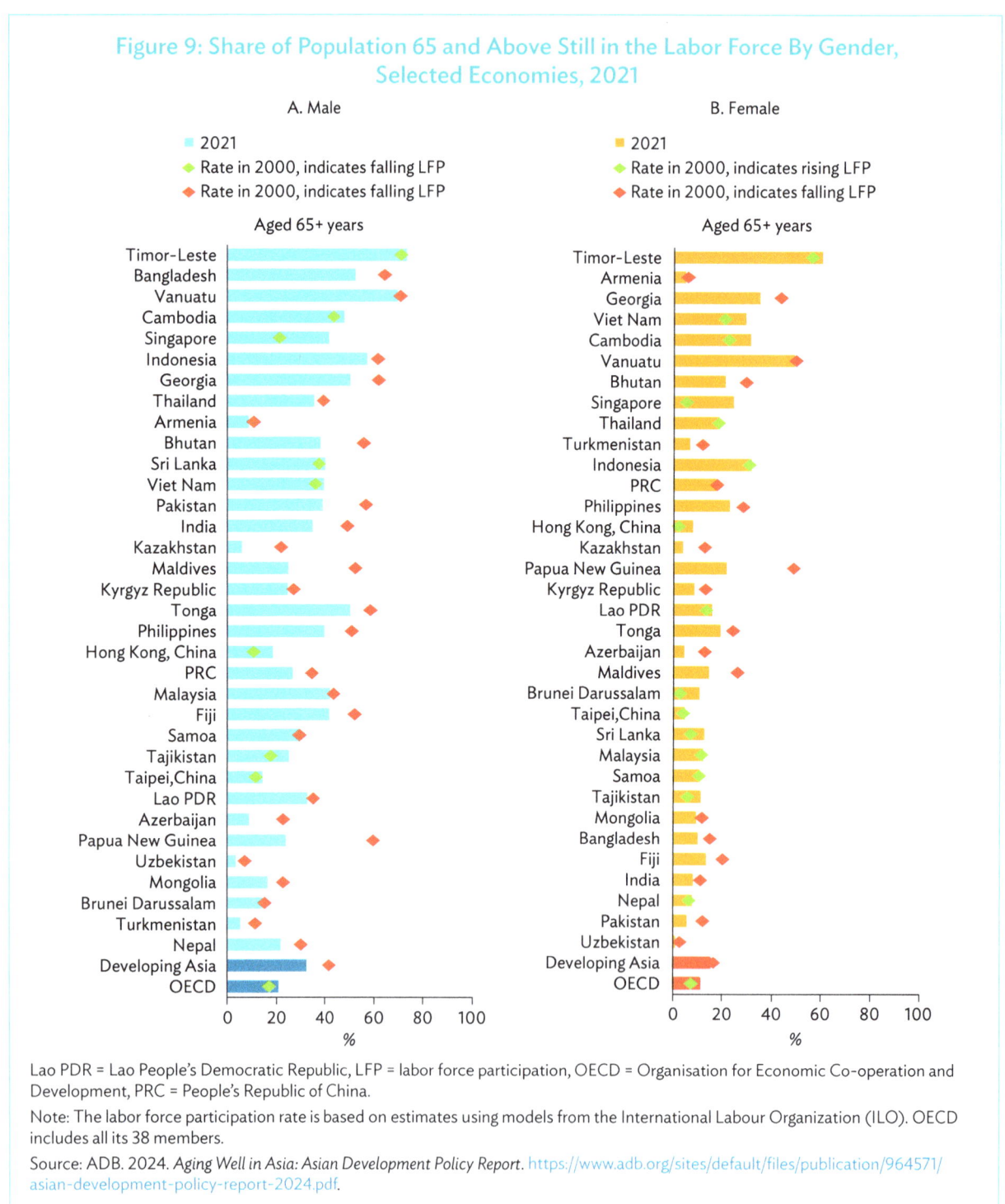

Figure 9: Share of Population 65 and Above Still in the Labor Force By Gender, Selected Economies, 2021

Lao PDR = Lao People's Democratic Republic, LFP = labor force participation, OECD = Organisation for Economic Co-operation and Development, PRC = People's Republic of China.

Note: The labor force participation rate is based on estimates using models from the International Labour Organization (ILO). OECD includes all its 38 members.

Source: ADB. 2024. *Aging Well in Asia: Asian Development Policy Report*. https://www.adb.org/sites/default/files/publication/964571/asian-development-policy-report-2024.pdf.

The digital transition generates new categories of workers that need access to social protection.
Traditionally, work has provided security if people are formally employed. Formal jobs are a mechanism for rights and benefits, including for work-related injury or sickness, and retirement. This is rooted in standard assumptions of workers in a shared physical workplace performing interrelated jobs in proximity to one another and a working age of 15–64 years.

The standard social architecture of work, or "regular" employment, is being disrupted by megatrends. In the digitally enabled gig economy, a new organization and location of work has emerged through independent, task- and platform-based contracting. Gig work can increase employment levels, but not the number of "employees" contributing to benefits systems. If gig workers are self-employed, and not classified as employees of the platform that mediates their participation in the labor market, access to social protection can only be delivered through other ways than an employment relationship (Box 6).[75] Gig labor markets imply a restructuring beyond the traditional "bimodal" way of classifying workers, i.e., as formal and included in social protection, or informal and excluded.[76]

Box 6: Extending Social Protection Coverage to Self-Employed Gig Workers

Governments and the private sector are experimenting with new ways to provide protection to platform workers—boosting job quality—without requiring a transition to formality:

In the **Philippines**, ride-hailing platform Grab has partnered with government agencies to provide access to a contributory social security scheme for registered drivers, covering social insurance for retirement, disability, death, funeral, sickness, maternity, and work-related contingencies; health-care services such as assistance with hospital bills or medication; and savings programs and affordable housing financing.

Self-employed workers in the **People's Republic of China (PRC)** can access employment injury benefits under social insurance programs on a voluntary basis. The scheme is primarily employer-financed, based on industry risk categorization.

In **Thailand**, public pension is available to self-employed workers, based on voluntary monthly contributions matched by government contributions of 50%–100% depending on age of the worker.

Singapore is considering legislative change to include gig workers in social insurance provision. Work injury insurance and pension coverage is planned to be extended to food delivery and ride-hailing workers. Contributions to the Central Provident Fund, Singapore's main social security fund, will be compulsory for gig workers aged below 30 years and voluntary (opt-in) for those above 30 years.

Sources: (Philippines) Grab. 2022. Grab Philippines, SSS, PhilHealth, Pag-IBIG launches social protection program for driver- and delivery-partners. 15 November. https://www.grab.com/ph/press/others/grabphsocialprotection; ADB. 2023. Gig Economy Employment during the Pandemic: An Analysis of GrabFood Driver Experiences in the Philippines. *ADB Briefs*. No. 251. https://www.adb.org/sites/default/files/publication/894231/adb-brief-251-gig-economy-employment-pandemic-philippines.pdf; (PRC and Thailand) S. Merothra. 2022. Can Asia Assure Social Insurance for All Its Informal Workers? *Asia-Pacific Sustainable Development Journal*. Vol. 29, No. 2. November. https://www.unescap.org/sites/default/d8files/2022-11/APSDJ%20Vol.%2029%2C%20No.%202_pp%20155-185.pdf; (Singapore) C. Lin. 2022. Singapore's gig workers to get work injury, pension coverage. *Reuters*. 24 November. https://www.reuters.com/markets/asia/singapores-gig-workers-get-work-injury-pension-coverage-2022-11-24; C. Yong. 2022. Gig workers in Singapore to get basic protection including insurance and CPF from as early as 2024. *The Straits Times*. 24 November. https://www.straitstimes.com/singapore/platform-workers-to-be-insured-against-workplace-injuries-get-cpf-payments; Government of Singapore, Ministry of Manpower. What is the Central Provident Fund (CPF). https://www.mom.gov.sg/employment-practices/central-provident-fund/what-is-cpf.

---

[75] ILO and OECD. 2023. Providing Adequate and Sustainable Social Protection for Workers in the Gig and Platform Economy. *Technical Paper for the G20 Employment Working Group under the Indian Presidency*. https://www.ilo.org/publications/providing-adequate-and-sustainable-social-protection-workers-gig-and.

[76] Banco Interamericano de Desarrollo. https://www.youtube.com/watch?v=FFpRcoBxYV8. J. Gruber. 2022. Designing Benefits for Platform Workers. *Working Paper* 29736. National Bureau of Economic Research. https://www.nber.org/system/files/working_papers/w29736/w29736.pdf, and E.N. Ravizki and N.S.A. Purnami. 2023. Guardians of autonomy: A comparative analysis of safeguarding independent self-employed workers in Indonesia and Europe. *Cogent Social Sciences*. 9 (2). https://doi.org/10.1080/23311886.2023.2273956.

The green transition—or the impacts of climate change—create new demands on social protection systems. Climate change creates new dynamics of livelihoods vulnerabilities that need to be met by appropriate social assistance and insurance. Growing numbers of people in the region will be unable to meet their basic needs without external support:[77]

> "Climate change will severely exacerbate existing socioeconomic drivers of poverty in multiple ways. The most serious implications include the loss of livelihoods, food and water insecurity, infrastructural breakdown, and significant health challenges which will increase the depth and scale of poverty globally, including across the Asia-Pacific region."[78]

The demand for targeted support to manage climate-related risks and access climate-related opportunities coincides with possible constraints in governments' response capacity due to climate-induced GDP losses. Social protection systems are undergoing restructuring to help address new climate-related inequities and ensure a just transition, including for the most vulnerable people.[79] This includes mitigating the potential poverty impacts of climate change mitigation policies, for example, if carbon pricing increases the cost of transport, which in turn increases the cost of a household's consumption basket. The dual role of social protection to mitigate risks but as well as expand opportunities has new demands under the green transition. Support to learn and adopt behaviors and practices that facilitate adaptation toward climate-resilient livelihoods is central to a just transition.[80] An ADB framework highlights a three-pronged approach to social protection adapted for climate: (i) reduced risk, (ii) strengthened capacity to adapt, and (iii) enhanced residual risk management strategies to help recover from the adverse impacts of climate change and disaster-related shocks and stresses (Figure 10).

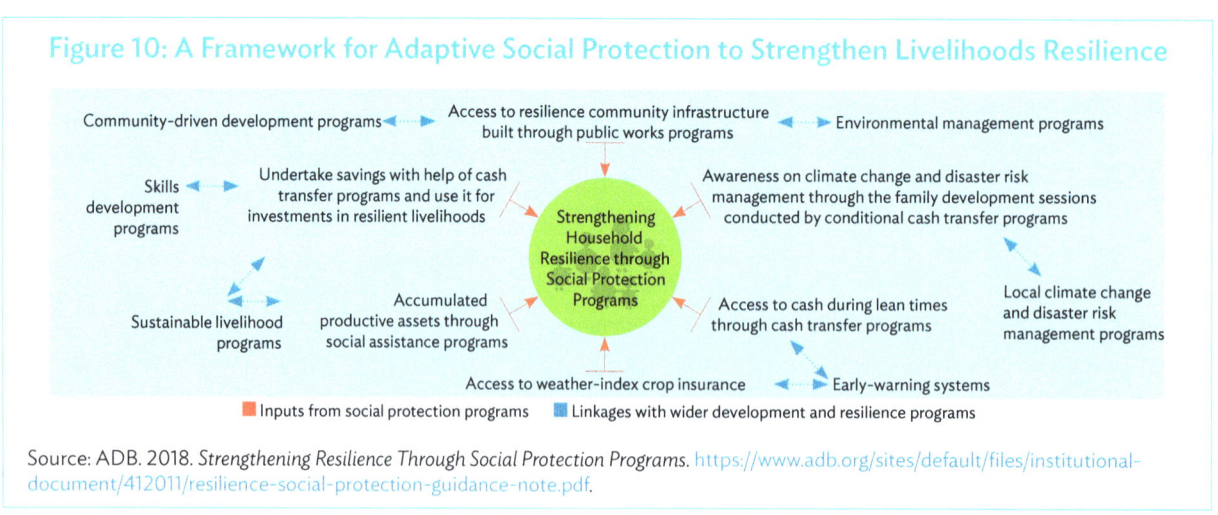

Figure 10: A Framework for Adaptive Social Protection to Strengthen Livelihoods Resilience

Source: ADB. 2018. *Strengthening Resilience Through Social Protection Programs*. https://www.adb.org/sites/default/files/institutional-document/412011/resilience-social-protection-guidance-note.pdf.

---

[77] C. Costella and A. McCord. 2023. *Rethinking Social Protection and Climate Change: The medium-term implications of climate change for social protection policy and programming in the Asia-Pacific region*. Government of Australia, Department of Foreign Affairs and Trade. https://www.dfat.gov.au/publications/development/rethinking-social-protection-and-climate-change-implications-climate-change-social-protection-policy-and-programming-asia-pacific-region.

[78] A. McCord. 2023. Why climate change will require a radical rethinking of social protection in the Asia-Pacific. 13 November. *Socialprotection.org*. https://socialprotection.org/discover/blog/why-climate-change-will-require-radical-rethinking-social-protection-asia-pacific.

[79] "A just transition means greening the economy in a way that is as fair and inclusive as possible to everyone concerned, creating decent work opportunities and leaving no one behind." ILO. 2024. Climate change and financing a just transition. 9 July. https://www.ilo.org/resource/other/climate-change-and-financing-just-transition.

[80] L. Schlogl, E. Weiss, and B. Prainsack. 2021. Constructing the 'Future of Work': An analysis of the policy discourse. *New Technology, Work and Employment*. 36. pp. 307–326. https://onlinelibrary.wiley.com/doi/10.1111/ntwe.12202.

Confluence: The Effects of Intersections

The ways the megatrends coexist and overlap ultimately determine the type and size of their effects. Typically, megatrends are studied in isolation, yet it is the combined effects of the three megatrends that will shape the future quantity and quality of jobs. For example, the energy industry needs to adapt to an aging workforce and optimize efficiency through digitalization, as well as invest in new, clean energy solutions. Health care is being revolutionized by digital capabilities, while facing new pressures from increasing longevity and environment-related illness—as well as the imperative to reduce its carbon footprint.

> Typically, megatrends are studied in isolation, yet it is the combined effects of the three megatrends that will shape the future quantity and quality of jobs.

Evidence is limited about the intersections of megatrends, which leaves uncertainty for governments in cost–benefit planning. The benefits of integrated assessment have been gaining recognition, including to inform public policy. For example, in 2000, the report of the UN Economist Network for the UN 75th Anniversary, *"Shaping The Trends Of Our Time,"* highlighted the gains from building policy based on the interlinkages between megatrends:

> *"Interlinkages among the megatrends mean that policies meant to steer one can influence others. Impact may go in any direction, but recognizing the connections offers the possibility to realize co-benefits, where positive impacts in one area result from an intervention to generate positive change in another. Not only are such policy interventions more effective, but they can also create mutually reinforcing changes that achieve significantly greater overall impacts."*[81]

This is in line with a broader shift toward better understanding of the complexity of development challenges and the need for integrated solutions.[82] Yet, even if recognition is growing, analytical gaps persist.[83] Table 3 maps some key linkages between megatrends, as discussed in the literature. These linkages are focused on labor demand—the main variable of interest in this study. In practice, the relevance and intensity of different intersections will vary by country or area.

---

[81] UN. 2020. *Shaping the Trends of Our Time.* https://www.un.org/development/desa/publications/wp-content/uploads/sites/10/2020/09/20-124-UNEN-75Report-2-1.pdf.

[82] For example, the latest edition of the Asia-Pacific SDG Partnership Report by UNESCAP, UNDP, and ADB focuses on how climate change interacts with other crises, such as the ongoing effects of the COVID-19 pandemic and cost-of-living crisis, to impact poverty and hunger in the region: ADB. People and Planet: Addressing the Interlinked Challenges of Climate Change, Poverty and Hunger in Asia and the Pacific. 20 February 2024. https://www.adb.org/news/events/people-planet-addressing-interlinked-challenges#:~:text=This%20edition%20of%20the%20Asia.

[83] For example, this 2023 analysis of megatrends by PwC concludes that "it's the interaction between these Megatrends that makes them particularly hard to deal with," but analyzes each megatrend separately. PwC. 2022. *Megatrends: Five global shifts reshaping the world we live in.* https://www.pwc.com/gx/en/issues/assets/pdf/pwc-megatrends-october-2022.pdf.

Table 3: Key Linkages Between Megatrends Affecting Labor Demand

Demographic transition ↔ Digital transition		
Automation can offset the negative effects of population aging on productivity.[a]	Job automation can help overcome labor shortages in the face of an aging population.[b]	Innovation in health tech will help tackle medical and other challenges associated with longevity, creating and disrupting jobs.
Growth in the gig economy increases demand for workers who prioritize flexibility, including younger and older workers.	Digitalization of work favors younger digital native workers, yet assistive technologies in the workplace can also enable longer working lives, e.g., for degraded eyesight or physical mobility.	Digitalization of training expands access for continuous upgrading of skills in line with changing workplace demands ("lifelong learning")—assuming digital access/connectivity.
Digital transition ↔ Green transition		
Digitalization is a route for less carbon-intensive production, consumption and work.[c] For example, remote working cuts GHG emissions through reduced travel.	The transition to renewable energy requires both digital and power electronics technologies in electric power generation, transmission, and consumption—shifting labor demand.[d]	Digital innovations can help support climate-vulnerable workers. For example, AI-powered applications for farmers.
Digitalization holds promise for expansion of climate-adaptive social protection. Yet, good design is essential to protect against risks of entrenched vulnerability exclusion, data privacy, and service transparency.[e]		
Green transition ↔ Demographic transition		
If population growth slows, energy consumption falls, yet aging—and smaller household sizes—contribute to moderately increased energy consumption per capita—inducing shifts in labor markets.[f]	As populations grow, demand for food increases and consumption preferences can change, with implications for jobs in agriculture (as well as use of natural resources).	Displacement of livelihoods in climate-affected locations increases rural–urban migration flows, affecting consumption and employment patterns.
Climate change makes work conditions more challenging, especially for older (and other vulnerable) workers exposed to increasing heat waves and other stressors.	New jobs in the green economy help young people find work aligned with their environmental and social priorities.	

GHG = greenhouse gas.

[a] A. F. Gravina and M. Lanzafame. 2023. Demography, Growth, and Robots in Advanced and Emerging Economies. *ADB Economics Working Paper Series*. No. 701. ADB. https://www.adb.org/sites/default/files/publication/922246/ewp-701-demography-growth-robots.pdf.

[b] D. Acemoglu and P. Restrepo. 2022. Demographics and automation. *The Review of Economic Studies*. 89 (1). pp. 1–44. https://doi.org/10.1093/restud/rdab031.

[c] Huawei. 2022. *Digital First Economy*. https://www-file.huawei.com/-/media/corp2020/pdf/tech-insights/1/huawei_dfe_whitepaper_asia_pacific.pdf?la=en.

[d] WEF. 2023. *3 Strategies for Delivering Digital Transformation in the Asia-Pacific*. https://www.weforum.org/agenda/2023/01/3-strategies-for-delivering-digital-infrasturcture-in-the-asia-pacific/.

[e] C. Lowe. 2022. The digitalisation of social protection before and since the onset of Covid-19: Opportunities, challenges and lessons. *ODI Working Paper*. https://odi.cdn.ngo/media/documents/ODI_Working_paper_Digitalisation_of_social_protection.pdf; T. Bowen et al. 2020. Adaptive Social Protection Building Resilience to Shocks. International Bank for Reconstruction and Development/The World Bank. https://openknowledge.worldbank.org/server/api/core/bitstreams/7ab2af13-08ca-5b10-b08b-268e6519eb15/content.

[f] C. Deuster et al. 2023. *Demography and Climate Change*. Publications Office of the European Union. https://publications.jrc.ec.europa.eu/repository/handle/JRC133580.

3 Policy Considerations

The Role of Policy and Markets

The megatrends shape labor demand through a combination of market forces and policy intervention. These two are linked. An enabling regulatory environment will encourage more risk-taking and investment by private actors. Conversely, progress can stall, for example if private sector investors or developers do not have confidence in future markets. It is how economies respond to megatrends that determines the consequences for the labor market. Megatrends have the potential to expand access to quality jobs, but also risk deepening fractures in the region's labor markets, notably increasing precarious informality.

The effects of megatrends are not predetermined; the policy agenda is an important determinant of outcomes. The fact that policy plays a determining role is important. It means that the impacts of megatrends can *in part* be controlled by the policy choices a government makes; i.e., the impacts are not just the by-product of the market alone. Policy interventions will significantly shape which direction an economy may take:

> *"The total employment effect of the digital revolution, while hard to foresee, is non-deterministic… Transiting to the digital future where more jobs will be created will not happen by default: it is a social and political choice."*[84]

The climate change agenda is arguably the most influenced by policy over markets. The perception of relative commitment to a global policy agenda to reduce carbon emissions frames private activity. Indeed, government climate policy is a driver of private investment through directly shaping investor risk appetite and behavior.[85]

The prevailing policy agenda related to megatrends is too narrow and siloed. First, policy dialogue tends to be mainly built from assessing megatrends separately. Second, it tends to center on skilling and social protection. These are two critical pillars of a policy response, and they are undergoing important updates in view of the implications of megatrends, as described briefly in Box 7. Yet, they are insufficient in the absence of jobs-specific interventions, focused on stimulating demand for quality jobs in inclusive and sustainable labor markets. Arguably, there has been an overemphasis on skilling as a policy response to megatrends. A recent review of future of work literature highlighted the following:

---

[84] ILO. 2021. *Changing demand for skills in digital economies and societies. Literature review and case studies from Low- and Middle-income Countries.* https://www.ilo.org/publications/changing-demand-skills-digital-economies-and-societies-literature-review.

[85] Z. Gao et al. 2023. When Governments Talk Climate, Investors Listen: Policies Can Drive Green Investments. Asian Development Blog. https://blogs.adb.org/blog/when-governments-talk-climate-investors-listen-policies-can-drive-green-investments.

> *"...Even matched skills may not guarantee job security in labour markets that diverge from full employment... (Re)Training strategies inevitably imply a promise of economic betterment which, failing to materialise, may well produce frustration (footnote 82)."*

Box 7: Skilling and Social Protection for the Triple Transition

Adapting to the triple transition, the skilling agenda is evolving toward lifelong learning ecosystems. These emphasize systems-level reform of human capital development at all stages, from early childhood teaching of foundational skills to mid- and late-career learning through employer partnerships. Skill development priorities are in frontier technical areas, such as care, digital, and green skills, as well as soft skills that emphasize the value of human labor over technology.

Similarly, the social protection agenda is also evolving under the triple transition. A key function of social protection is to enable workers to adapt to megatrends and transition into in-demand jobs. Activation and income replacement become higher priorities due to increased labor market churn.[a] Faced with demographic pressures, social protection is shifting toward a life-cycle approach, equipping people to make positive transitions through the evolving experiences of their (longer) working lives.[b] A major focus for the digital economy is reform of social security systems in order to include nonstandard forms of employment. Governments and employers are experimenting with innovative approaches to social insurance that are scalable, especially among informal workers (Box 6). For the green transition, adaptive modalities are another area of innovation that help climate-vulnerable households to be better prepared for shocks, to cope and to recover.

[a] Activation policies can include skills, matching/employment services, and job subsidies.
[b] In a life-cycle approach, social protection is designed to address the different risks and vulnerabilities that people face at different stages in life. Socialprotection.org. What is Social Protection? Lifecycle approach. https://socialprotection.org/learn/glossary/lifecycle-approach#:~:text=It%20reflects%20that%20individuals%20.

Preparing for the triple transition is best supported by an integrated policy approach. There are multiple complexities. Not only do the effects of the transitions overlap, but each interacts at the nexus of other related development challenges, such as poverty, inequality, or food insecurity. Integrating policy in this way places new demands on policy actors and requires new capabilities. It means better understanding the overlaps between megatrends and their implications, in order to maximize efficiencies and development impacts. Some of the implications will relate to setting policy priorities. Others will alter policy implementation in line with fast-paced and unpredictable shifts in labor demand.

Intersectional policymaking requires upgraded assessment tools that bring together key indicators across overlapping transitions. The triple transition calls for a new set of composite instruments capable of combining insights from the intersections of megatrends to identify opportunities for efficiency gains, impact multipliers, and crosscutting interventions. The World Risk Index provides an example, enabling cross-country comparison as well as in-country diagnostics. It is a multi-component index measuring countries' risk, exposure, vulnerability, susceptibility, coping capacities, and adaptive capacities, with indicators for each component across demographics (such as old age and young age dependency), digital (broadband and cellular penetration), and climate (populations affected by disasters), among other areas.[86]

The job gains from an integrated policy response to megatrends can be significant. ILO research modeled the employment effects of a "big push" policy scenario, combining care, digital, and green investments. The model simulated four scenarios based on assumptions of additional policy investments: a "green scenario," a "digital scenario," a "care scenario," and a "combined scenario" that combines the first three. If countries implement the combined scenario, by 2030 global GDP would rise by 4.2% and an additional 139 million jobs would be created, relative to a modeled baseline, i.e., compared with a business-as-usual scenario without the additional investments. It is mainly the care scenario that drives the job creation, accounting for almost three-fifths of the increase. The next largest contribution to employment comes from the green scenario, with the lowest number of jobs created through the digital scenario. The combined scenario induces a net uplift in GDP compared to implementing the three policy packages separately, potentially unlocking broad-based development impacts.[87]

An Intersectional Policy Approach

The following four policy shifts can help governments progress toward a more intersectional policymaking approach to maximize labor demand in the triple transition. The shifts aim to move beyond the established policy discourse related to megatrends. They explicitly put a jobs-rich transition at the forefront. They further provide an integrated policy frame, centered on managing the intersections between megatrends. This policy frame highlights the role of governments. It is noted that labor markets are shaped by a range of actors, including governments, employers, training providers, and workers, and that policy responses to megatrends require multistakeholder collaboration and social dialogue.[88] Governments have comparative advantage in convening and in shaping a constructive policy narrative.

---

[86] Nine out of the top 15 most at-risk countries in the world are in Asia and the Pacific. WorldRiskReport 2023. https://weltrisikobericht.de/wp-content/uploads/2024/01/WorldRiskReport_2023_english_online.pdf.

[87] ILO. 2022. *Global Employment Trends for Youth 2022*. https://www.ilo.org/wcmsp5/groups/public/---dgreports/---dcomm/---publ/documents/publication/wcms_853321.pdf. In the green-only scenario, investments in climate change adaptation, mitigation, and greening would lead to net employment creation of 37 million jobs worldwide by 2030. This would represent 1% more jobs in 2030 than would be created without the investments, i.e., business as usual. In the digital-only scenario, increased investment could lead to net employment creation of 24 million jobs. In the care-only scenario, investment would lead to net employment creation of almost 80 million jobs, which would be 2.2% more than business as usual. The simple sum of these three scenarios is 141 million jobs created. The combined scenario (i.e., single estimation that includes the three areas of investment) is slightly lower, at 139 million jobs. This difference is due to interactions between the three areas, notably that the combined investment activity would lead to greater technological change and higher wages, which can reduce labor demand (i.e., intensity). The projections are conservative estimates of direct employment generation and do not capture indirect benefits.

[88] Social dialogue has a particularly formative role during times of socioeconomic disruption. See for example Dondi et al. 2020. *A government blueprint to adapt the ecosystem to the future of work*. McKinsey & Company. https://www.mckinsey.com/industries/public-sector/our-insights/a-government-blueprint-to-adapt-the-ecosystem-to-the-future-of-work.

Policy shift 1: Create a jobs-centered approach to megatrends.

Governments need an intentional and coordinated jobs-centered policy agenda for the triple transition. The policy objective should shift from economic growth per se, to inclusive and sustainable growth centered on quality jobs for productivity. A jobs-centered policy agenda will span multiple policy areas, such as finance, welfare, education, environment, and transport. Employment outcomes need to be explicitly defined, in line with national priorities, across job creation, job quality, and job access, through policies for digital interconnectivity, environmental sustainability, and demographic inclusivity. Job creation means demand-side policy intervention to enable and stimulate the generation of decent employment. The key job-quality issue relates to improving quality deficits in informal work. Job access requires a focus on transition support to maximize economic inclusion in the triple transition.

Policy example: Korean New Deal, 2020 (New Deal 2.0 updated 2021)

The Government of the Republic of Korea developed a coordinated policy agenda to address three types of structural change, with an explicit focus on employment. The agenda combines a Digital New Deal, a Green New Deal, and a Human New Deal. The latter includes "radical transformation of economic and social structures, and the consequent reform of the labor market" in response to megatrends. The intentional role of policy is acknowledged in addressing the "threat" of "shrinking traditional jobs and emerging new forms of work" as well as the "opportunity" of "new jobs from the Digital and Green New Deals." Job creation targets are set for each of the three pillars as part of the investment strategies. Policy on Employment and Social Safety Nets includes "Ensuring livelihoods and employment stability for those not covered by employment insurance."[89]

Policy shift 2: Strengthen capacity to anticipate changing labor demand.

Policy systems and institutions for the triple transition need to be agile and flexible in step with evolving labor market demand. The new normal in policymaking is uncertainty. Navigating the triple transition means dealing in scenarios and forecasts.[90] This puts an emphasis on data collection and analysis: collecting the right data to provide useful signals of future directions in the labor market; and smart analytics that can generate feedback loops geared to the pace of change. Adaptive implementation and evaluation approaches become important tools of government in support of building resilient labor markets. Public–private cooperation can generate useful knowledge and resources for experimentation.[91] The extent of anticipatory planning for change will be critical, not least because changes in labor demand lag changes in growth.[92] The right data can also help strengthen understanding of the combined impacts of megatrends and potential efficiencies in integrated solutions.

---

[89] Government of the Republic of Korea. 2020. The Korean New Deal: National Strategy for a Great Transformation. https://english.moef.go.kr/skin/doc.html?fn=Korean%20New%20Deal.pdf&rs=/result/upload/mini/2020/07; OECD. Korean New Deal. https://infrastructure-toolkit.oecd.org/wp-content/uploads/Korea_NewDeal.pdf.

[90] Job modeling typically assumes sector sizes are fixed and that the tasks required in each occupation are unchanged, which is not the case.

[91] See for example: OECD Reviews of Innovation Policy: Germany 2022: Building Agility for Successful Transitions. https://www.oecd.org/en/publications/oecd-reviews-of-innovation-policy-germany-2022_50b32331-en.html.

[92] See for example: C. Öner. Unemployment: The Curse of Joblessness. IMF. https://www.imf.org/external/pubs/ft/fandd/basics/unemploy.htm.

Policy example. Centre for Strategic Futures, Strategy Group, Prime Minister's Office, Singapore

Singapore has a long history in building capabilities in strategic foresight, defined as the "structured and explicit exploration of multiple futures in order to inform decision-making." A central Centre for Strategic Futures coordinates activity in strategic foresight units across government. It has developed a range of anticipatory policy tools and instruments, including to account for unlikely events and consequences, for example so-called "black swan" events.[93] Monitoring is an important feature of the policy suite, including early-warning systems, "to analyze risks, monitor and warn of potential critical threats, and build a response capability to these threats." Linked to employment issues, a key partner to the Centre for Strategic Futures is the Ministry of Manpower's Risk Management and Futures Group.[94]

Policy shift 3: Understand distributional impacts of megatrends on people and jobs.

The triple transition calls for strengthened policy capabilities in shaping human-centered responses. The distributional impacts of the triple transition are significant, with multiple risks of entrenched and newly generated inequalities. National-level data mask the localized, and ultimately, personal nature of how the triple transition shapes risk and opportunity. Impacts are specific to the people and sectors in individual communities. Governments need policy approaches that assess and cater to the differentiated experiences of individual workers faced with job disruptions due to megatrends, supporting all workers to transition into available and in-demand quality jobs. This recommendation is in line with the shift in provision of public employment services to be more personalized and tailored to individualized needs. It also places new demands on data gathering and analysis, like Policy shift 2. Given the increased threat to labor market inclusion and job security, especially among marginalized groups, policies need to account directly for protecting social cohesion as people transition and adapt.[95]

Policy example: Network Readiness Index, Portulans Institute and University of Oxford Saïd Business School, global

A collaborative initiative launched in 2002 at the WEF illustrates how research efforts about megatrends are evolving to take more account of individuals' capacities, in order to inform people-centered policy. The Network Readiness Index combines measures across Technology, People, Governance, and Impact, to evaluate 134 economies on their readiness for the digital transition. The People pillar includes assessment of citizens' digital access, specifically "individual technological utilization and their capacity to engage in the networked economy." This pillar also includes how businesses and governments deploy and enable technology adoption. Table 4 lists the highest and lowest ranking economies by people in Asia and the Pacific.

---

[93] Defined as "high-impact event that is difficult to predict under normal circumstances but that in retrospect appears to have been inevitable." https://www.britannica.com/topic/black-swan-event.
[94] OECD. 2021. *Foresight and Anticipatory Governance in Practice. Lessons in Effective Foresight Institutionalization.* https://www.oecd.org/strategic-foresight/ourwork/Foresight_and_Anticipatory_Governance.pdf and CDF. n.d. *Our Approach.* https://www.csf.gov.sg/our-work/our-approach/.
[95] European Investment Bank. 2021. Chapter 10: The impact of digitalisation and climate change policies on social cohesion. In *Building a smart and green Europe in the COVID-19 era.* https://www.eib.org/attachments/efs/economic_investment_report_2020_chapter10_en.pdf.

Table 4: Individuals' Readiness for the Digital Economy—Network Readiness Index People Ranking of Highest- and Lowest-Performing Economies in the Region

Highest ranking (Highest first)	Lowest ranking (Lowest first)
Republic of Korea (1)	Nepal (122)
Japan (3)	Tajikistan (119)
People's Republic of China (5)	Cambodia (104)
Singapore (6)	Kyrgyz Republic (101)
Australia (13)	Lao People's Democratic Republic (98)
New Zealand (23)	Mongolia (92)
Thailand (34)	Bangladesh (90)
Hong Kong, China (35)	Pakistan (89)
Malaysia (48)	Uzbekistan (88)
Kazakhstan (49)	Sri Lanka (86)

Source: Network Readiness Index, Portulans Institute, 2023. Portulans Institute. 2023. *A Crisis of the Digital Age?* https://download.networkreadinessindex.org/reports/nri_2023.pdf.

Policy shift 4: Focus on productivity enhancement of informal workers.

Success of the policy response to the triple transition should be measured by improvements to the productivity of the majority informal workforce of the region. Without intentional policy action, the combined effects of the megatrends may worsen labor underutilization and low productivity in the region. Especially in the care and digital economies, new jobs may (continue to) be informal, unprotected, and precarious. It is important to avoid reform packages that will only benefit more educated and experienced workers. These will not reach the majority of the workforce, nor tackle the underlying constraints to better productivity performance in the region. The triple transition is prompting new thinking around how to unlock labor productivity in markets dominated by informality and the services sector, as in Asia;[96] especially in view of the potential for white-collar services occupations to be automated.[97] Controlling technologies' effects on labor through targeted policy intervention can influence productivity. For example, governments can promote applications of technologies that maximize human labor and productivity, and benefit in particular the low-skilled:

> *"Today it is widely recognized that governments have a critical role in fostering green technologies. Given the importance of promoting good jobs, it could be argued that they have an equally critical role in promoting labor-friendly technologies… Just like green innovation, labor-friendly innovation is a global public good."*[98]

---

[96] M. Helble, T. Long, and T. Le. 2019. Sectoral and Skill Contributions to Labor Productivity in Asia. *ADBI Working Paper*. No. 929. Asian Development Bank Institute. https://www.adb.org/sites/default/files/publication/489461/adbi-wp929.pdf.

[97] CSAE. n.d. *AI and Services-Led Growth: Evidence from Indian Job Adverts*. https://www.csae.ox.ac.uk/ai-and-services-led-growth-evidence-from-indian-job-adverts.

[98] D. Rodrik and J.E. Stiglitz. 2024. *A New Growth Strategy for Developing Nations*. IEA-ERIA Project on the New Global Economic Order. https://drodrik.scholar.harvard.edu/sites/scholar.harvard.edu/files/dani-rodrik/files/a_new_growth_strategy_for_developing_nations.pdf.

Policy example: ASEAN Labor Productivity Index

ASEAN is placing policy emphasis on labor productivity, with the aim that "higher productivity promotes inclusive growth." Following analytical work, a next step is the development of an ASEAN Labor Productivity Index to understand better the input variables that drive labor productivity, noting the significance of human capital. This will improve policy targeting to address in-country gaps and cross-country inequities. It includes an explicit focus on "those who are employed but underutilized and those who are at the fringe of economic activities. These include workers in micro, small, and medium enterprises (MSMEs), those working in the informal economy, women undertaking activities in households or family-owned concerns but not in the formal labour force, and persons with disabilities."[99]

The Context Effect

Policy priorities depend on the extent of penetration of megatrends in a particular country or area. In some cases, the recommendations will imply new priorities and competences. Other governments will already be moving in these recommended directions, but need to develop more advanced knowledge or capabilities. If a place in particular is heavily affected by one or more megatrends, related priorities will necessarily be given more weight in the policy mix. For example, in those economies highly exposed to climate risks, such as the Pacific island countries, human- and livelihoods-centered environmental preservation may become the primary goal.

"Readiness" of the policy and investment environment affects a government's capacity for response. Various rankings are developed to monitor readiness for the digital and green transitions in particular, yet overall, readiness is also affected by crosscutting capabilities—such as those outlined above—which are more challenging to measure. There is wide variation across the region, correlated closely to stage of economic development. Figure 11 shows this variance in "technology adoption," a key component of digital readiness.[100]

---

[99] ASEAN Secretariat. 2021. *Regional Study on Labour Productivity in ASEAN.* https://asean.org/wp-content/uploads/Regional-Study-on-Labor-Productivity-in-ASEAN_R05_Kirimok.pdf.

[100] Technology adoption is the demand for digital products and services.

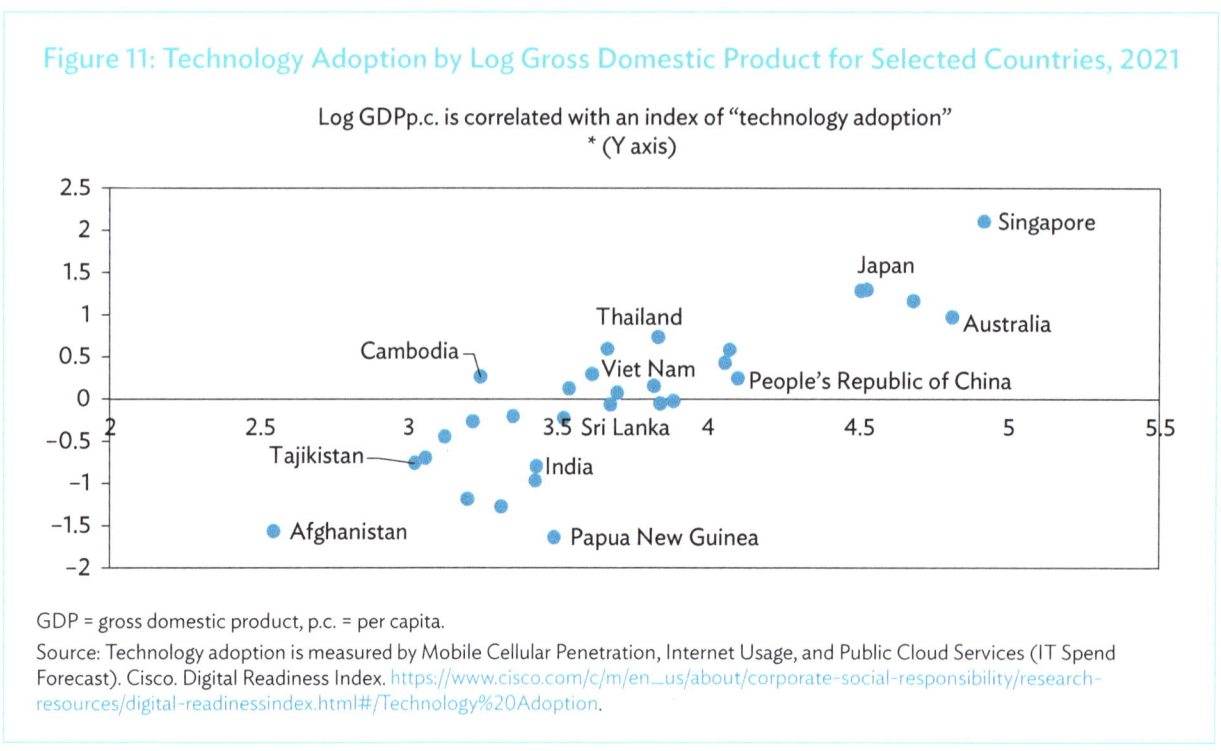

GDP = gross domestic product, p.c. = per capita.
Source: Technology adoption is measured by Mobile Cellular Penetration, Internet Usage, and Public Cloud Services (IT Spend Forecast). Cisco. Digital Readiness Index. https://www.cisco.com/c/m/en_us/about/corporate-social-responsibility/research-resources/digital-readinessindex.html#/Technology%20Adoption.

Policy design and implementation should be flexible to the differentiated diffusion of megatrends and adaptation capacity among countries. This is increasingly evident in policy guidance related to the triple transition, although typically it will relate to a single transition. For example, ILO's *Guidelines on Green Employment Diagnostics for Just Transitions* highlight flexibility:

> *"Economies vary by type, extent of vulnerability and adaptive capacity: this necessitates that the framework ought to be sufficiently flexible to accommodate these differences. Key variabilities across developing countries include (among others) differences in employment parameters, low/medium/high levels of climate risk exposure and vulnerabilities, differences in macro-fiscal stabilities, and differences in adaptive capacities at the institutional and micro levels."*[101]

---

[101] ILO. 2023. *Guidelines on Green Employment Diagnostics for Just Transitions*. https://genesis.imgix.net/uploads/files/CFE-ILO-report.pdf.

4 Conclusion

This report assesses the labor market impacts of three megatrends in Asia and the Pacific and concludes that adequate policy response can only be achieved through more focus on how the megatrends overlap and intersect. Typically, megatrends are studied in isolation, yet it is their combined effects that will shape the future quantity and quality of jobs. Based on mapping some key linkages between megatrends related to labor demand, a new approach to policymaking for the triple transition is proposed, centered on four policy shifts that will help governments adopt a more intersectional policy approach to address the labor market impacts of megatrends.

The net employment effects of the triple transition are expected to be positive. Job estimates vary depending if they account for indirect and induced job loss or creation in value chain multiplier effects. Overall, more jobs will be transformed than lost or created. Of the three emergent labor market sectors, the care economy is forecast to be the largest creator of jobs. All jobs will be affected by greening and digitalization. Triple transition jobs will generally be higher skilled. While technologies can displace labor, mainly they will improve productivity, which for individuals can increase wages and job satisfaction, and at the macro level can induce positive employment effects.

However, the megatrends pose new challenges for labor market inclusion. There is significant heterogeneity in the ways in which the megatrends are taking shape across the region, as well as their potential to reshape labor demand. Inequities arise between and within countries, and for individuals, depending on capabilities to cope with change and to adapt to access new opportunities. When redundant jobs are substituted, and new jobs created, temporal and spatial misalignments are common, i.e., the creation of new jobs usually lags behind the destruction of old ones, and occurs in a different location. This creates new dynamics around which communities and workers can transition into jobs.

The job impacts of the triple transition depend on the policy choices governments make. The three transitions exert a combination of market forces and policy incentives on the structures of production and consumption, which influences which jobs are in demand. Policy plays a determining role in shaping future outcomes. Without intentional action, the job benefits of the triple transition will not be realized. Governments and other stakeholders can create an environment that unlocks jobs-rich change and, furthermore, that targets better job quality and productivity, including for the majority of workers in the region who remain in low-skilled, informal work despite higher growth rates. Beyond a dedicated jobs- and productivity-focused agenda, governments will also need new capabilities for agile and flexible policymaking conducive to the conditions of transformation and uncertainty.

Policy analysis and intervention are shifting toward more integrated approaches, yet more work is needed to address the overlapping effects of megatrends. This report highlights examples of development institutions and national governments adopting new priorities and new tools in order to address—and, indeed, to leverage—intersections between megatrends. These include coordinated employment-centered policymaking across green, digital, and human agendas (Republic of Korea), focus on labor productivity (ASEAN), and anticipatory policy instruments (Singapore). More assistance to evaluate different approaches, share knowledge, and build capacity will help equip governments for policymaking in the triple transition.

References

ADB. 2018. *Asian Development Outlook (ADO) 2018: How Technology Affects Jobs.* https://www.adb.org/sites/default/files/publication/411666/ado2018.pdf.

ADB. 2018. *STRATEGY 2030: Achieving a Prosperous, Inclusive, Resilient, and Sustainable Asia and the Pacific.* https://www.adb.org/sites/default/files/institutional-document/435391/strategy-2030-main-document.pdf.

ADB. 2021. *Capturing the Digital Economy: A Proposed Measurement Framework and Its Applications.* https://www.adb.org/sites/default/files/publication/722366/capturing-digital-economy-measurement-framework.pdf.

ADB. 2021. *Reaping the Benefits of Industry 4.0 through Skills Development in High-Growth Industries in Southeast Asia: Insights from Cambodia, Indonesia, the Philippines, and Viet Nam.* https://www.adb.org/sites/default/files/publication/671711/industry-skills-development-southeast-asia.pdf.

ADB. 2022. *The Social Protection Indicator for Asia: Tracking Developments in Social Protection.* https://www.adb.org/sites/default/files/publication/849591/social-protection-indicator-asia-tracking-developments.pdf.

ADB. 2023. *Asian Economic Integration Report 2023: Trade, Investments, and Climate Change in Asia and the Pacific.* https://www.adb.org/sites/default/files/publication/859946/asian-economic-integration-report-2023.pdf.

ADB. 2023. *Job Matching for Youth in Asia and the Pacific: A Transitions Approach for Positive Labor Market Pathways.* https://www.adb.org/sites/default/files/publication/923096/job-matching-youth-asia-pacific.pdf.

ADB, UNESCAP, and UNDP. 2023. *Delivering on the Sustainable Development Goals through Solutions at the Energy, Food, and Finance Nexus.* https://www.adb.org/sites/default/files/institutional-document/870986/2023-asia-pacific-sdg-partnership-report.pdf.

Bradley, C., J. Seong, S.Smit, and L. Woetzel. 2022. On the cusp of a new era? *McKinsey & Company Discussion Paper.* https://www.mckinsey.com/capabilities/risk-and-resilience/our-insights/on-the-cusp-of-a-new-era.

Burgess, R., S. Caria, T. Dobermann, and A. Saggese. 2023. *Innovation, growth, and the environment.* International Growth Centre. https://www.theigc.org/sites/default/files/2023-11/IGCP10455-Sustainable-growth-white-paper-INT-230922-WEB.pdf.

Chacaltana, J., F. Bonnet, and J. M. Garcia. 2022. Growth, economic structure and informality. *ILO Working Papers.* https://www.ilo.org/static/english/intserv/working-papers/wp069/index.html#ID0ED1EM.

Davis, J. B. and R. McMaster. 2020. A road not taken? A brief history of care in economic thought. *The European Journal of the History of Economic Thought*. 4 February. https://www.tandfonline.com/doi/abs/10.1080/09672567.2020.1720767.

Datta, N., C. Rong, S. Singh, C. Stinshoff, N. Iacob, N. S. Nigatu, M. Nxumalo, and L. Klimaviciute. 2023. *Working Without Borders: The Promise and Peril of Online Gig Work*. World Bank. https://openknowledge.worldbank.org/entities/publication/ebc4a7e2-85c6-467b-8713-e2d77e954c6c.

Fankhauser, S., A. Kazaglis, and S. Srivastav. 2017. Green Growth Opportunities for Asia. *ADB Economics Working Paper Series*. No. 508. ADB. https://www.adb.org/sites/default/files/publication/224391/ewp-508.pdf.

Food and Agriculture Organization of the United Nations (FAO). 2021. *Climate-smart agriculture case studies 2021 – Projects from around the world*. https://doi.org/10.4060/cb5359en.

Gmyrek, P., J. Berg, and D. Bescond. 2023. Generative AI and jobs: A global analysis of potential effects on job quantity and quality. *ILO Working Paper*. 96. https://www.ilo.org/wcmsp5/groups/public/---dgreports/---inst/documents/publication/wcms_890761.pdf.

Gravina, A. F. and M. Lanzafame. 2023. Demography, Growth, and Robots in Advanced and Emerging Economies. *ADB Economics Working Paper Series*. No. 701. ADB. https://www.adb.org/sites/default/files/publication/922246/ewp-701-demography-growth-robots.pdf.

Hovhannisyan, S., V. Montalva-Talledo, T. Remick, C. Rodríguez-Castelán, and K. Stamm. 2022. Global Job Quality. Evidence from Wage Employment across Developing Countries. *World Bank Policy Research Working Paper*. 10134. https://documents1.worldbank.org/curated/en/099815508012237346/pdf/IDU09ac855b6033b20401e0b7d20c77cc771201c.pdf.

ILO. 2005. *Social protection as a productive factor*. https://www.ilo.org/sites/default/files/wcmsp5/groups/public/@ed_protect/@soc_sec/documents/publication/wcms_secsoc_10291.pdf.

ILO. 2018. *Care Work and Care Jobs for the Future Of Decent Work*. https://www.ilo.org/wcmsp5/groups/public/---dgreports/---dcomm/---publ/documents/publication/wcms_633135.pdf.

ILO. 2019. *Working on a WARMER planet: The impact of heat stress on labour productivity and decent work*. https://www.ilo.org/sites/default/files/wcmsp5/groups/public/@dgreports/@dcomm/@publ/documents/publication/wcms_711919.pdf.

ILO. 2020. *Global Employment Trends for Youth 2020: Technology and the future of jobs*. https://www.ilo.org/wcmsp5/groups/public/---dgreports/---dcomm/---publ/documents/publication/wcms_737648.pdf.

ILO. 2022. *Asia–Pacific Employment and Social Outlook: Rethinking sectoral strategies for a human-centred future of work*. https://www.ilo.org/wcmsp5/groups/public/---dgreports/---dcomm/---publ/documents/publication/wcms_862410.pdf.

ILO. 2022. *Global Employment Trends for Youth 2022: Investing in transforming futures for young people*. https://www.ilo.org/wcmsp5/groups/public/---dgreports/---dcomm/---publ/documents/publication/wcms_853321.pdf.

IRENA and ILO. 2022. *Renewable Energy and Jobs: Annual Review 2022*. https://www.ilo.org/wcmsp5/groups/public/---dgreports/---dcomm/documents/publication/wcms_856649.pdf.

IPCC. 2022. Chapter 8: Poverty, Livelihoods and Sustainable Development. In H. Pörtner et al., eds. *Climate Change 2022: Impacts, Adaptation and Vulnerability*. https://www.ipcc.ch/report/ar6/wg2/chapter/chapter-8/.

Lowe, C., A. McCord, and R. Beazley. 2021. National cash transfer responses to Covid-19. *ODI Working Paper*. 610. https://cdn.odi.org/media/documents/ODI_Implementation_final.pdf.

Mason, A. and R. Lee. 2022. Six Ways Population Change Will Affect the Global Economy. *Population and Development Review*. Vol. 48, Issue 1. https://onlinelibrary.wiley.com/doi/10.1111/padr.12469.

OECD. 2015. *Universal Basic Skills: What Countries Stand to Gain*. OECD Publishing. https://doi.org/10.1787/9789264234833-en.

OECD. 2017. *Employment Implications of Green Growth: Linking jobs, growth and green policies*. https://issuu.com/oecd.publishing/docs/employment-implications-of-green-gr.

OECD. 2019. *OECD Employment Outlook 2019. The Future of Work*. Paris. https://www.oecd.org/en/publications/oecd-employment-outlook-2019_9ee00155-en.html.

OECD. 2023. *Job Creation and Local Economic Development 2023: Bridging the Great Green Divide*. OECD Publishing. https://doi.org/10.1787/21db61c1-en.

Peng, I. 2019. The Care Economy: a new research framework. *LIEPP Working Paper*. https://sciencespo.hal.science/hal-03456901/document.

Schlogl, L., E. Weiss, and B. Prainsack. 2021. Constructing the 'Future of Work': An analysis of the policy discourse. *New Technology, Work and Employment*. 36. https://onlinelibrary.wiley.com/doi/10.1111/ntwe.12202.

Seong, J., C. Bradley, N. Leung, L. Woetzel, K. Ellingrud, G. Kumra, and P. Wang. 2023. *Asia on the cusp of a new era*. Mckinsey Global Institute. 22 September. https://www.mckinsey.com/mgi/our-research/asia-on-the-cusp-of-a-new-era.

Solutions for Youth Employment (S4YE). 2018. *Digital Jobs for Youth: Young Women in the Digital Economy*. World Bank Group. https://www.s4ye.org/sites/default/files/2018-11/S4YE%20Digital%20Jobs%20Report%20-%20FINAL%20%28For%20Printing%29.pdf.

The Asia Foundation. 2022. *Toward a Resilient Care Ecosystem in Asia and the Pacific: Promising Practices, Lessons Learned, and Pathways for Action on Decent Care Work*. https://asiafoundation.org/wp-content/uploads/2023/01/Towards-A-Resilient-Care-Ecosystem-in-Asia-and-the-Pacific.pdf.

UNESCAP. 2023. *Asia and the Pacific SDG Progress Report 2023*. https://www.unescap.org/kp/2023/asia-and-pacific-sdg-progress-report-2023#.

van der Wijst, K. et al. 2023. New damage curves and multimodel analysis suggest lower optimal temperature. *Nature Climate Change*. 13, 434–441. 23 March. https://doi.org/10.1038/s41558-023-01636-1.

World Bank. 2012. *World Development Report 2013: Jobs*. https://documents.worldbank.org/en/publication/documents-reports/documentdetail/263351468330025810/world-development-report-2013-jobs.

World Bank. 2020. *Scaling Up Social Assistance Payments as Part of the COVID-19 Pandemic Response*. https://thedocs.worldbank.org/en/doc/655201595885830480-0090022020/original/WBG2PxScalingupSocialAssistancePaymentsasPartoftheCovid19PandemicResponse.pdf.

World Bank. 2020. *The Human Capital Index 2020 Update: Human Capital in the Time of COVID-19*. https://openknowledge.worldbank.org/entities/publication/93f8fbc6-4513-58e7-82ec-af4636380319.

World Economic Forum. *The Future of Jobs Report 2023*. https://www.weforum.org/publications/the-future-of-jobs-report-2023/.